R` for
Sea Anglers
by Andrew Simpson

Illustrations by the Author

© Andrew Simpson 2008
First Published 2008
The Royal Yachting Association
RYA House, Ensign Way, Hamble
Southampton SO31 4YA
Tel: 0845 345 0400
Fax: 0845 345 0329
E-mail: publications@rya .org.uk
Web: www.rya.org.uk
ISBN: 978-1-905104-57-4
RYA Order Code: G50

Totally Chlorine
Free

Sustainable
Forests

A CIP record of this book is available from the British Library.

Note: While all reasonable care had been taken in the preparation
of this book, the publisher takes no responsibility for the use of the
methods or products or contracts described in the book.

Cover Design: Pete Galvin

Typesetting and Design: Kevin Slater

Proofreading and indexing: Alan Thatcher

Printed in China through World Print

FOREWORD

Sea Angling is a fascinating and absorbing pastime enjoyed by countless people. For many the pleasure of catching fish from headlands, beaches, and piers is satisfying enough, but fishing from a boat broadens the opportunities and brings a whole new dimension to the process.

For those anglers who seek to extend their horizons by using a boat, simply buying it and launching it whenever the opportunity presents itself would seem to be simple enough. Not so. The minute you go to sea, you enter a world where there are many pleasures but also attendant risks.

No sensible person should go to sea unprepared. There are many techniques and skills to be acquired, some of which are an absolute must. The sea can be a dangerous place, and you can feel very isolated once more than a few hundred yards off the shore. If things go wrong there's no breakdown service to call upon and, with the changeable weather we experience, small inconveniences can sometimes result in very frightening circumstances.

Boating is a recreation in its own right for many, and the sea angler needs to absorb a similar degree of knowledge to enjoy his or her fishing to the full. In this splendid book, all the information you could want concerning operating a small boat at sea is assembled in a way that will leave the reader feeling confident of having gained a good grasp of the essentials. From boat handling, understanding the ways of the sea, the equipment and its use and – of course – the essential subject of safety, each subject is covered in accessible detail. To read and absorb the material in this book will leave all sea anglers better equipped to face this challenging but satisfying environment.

Confidence at sea is important, and it's inevitable that the ability to use a boat properly and safely will extend the angler's horizons and lead, I predict, to bigger and better fish – and lots more of them.

Peter Chennell
RNLI Sea Safety Manager

INTRODUCTION

It's tempting to think of the sea as a place where anything goes. Once we leave harbour, there are few restrictions to torment us: no speed limits, traffic lights, parking prohibitions, 'keep off the grass' signs or any of the other pettifogging commands we must live with ashore. The personal freedom the sea offers is one of its strongest attractions and it regularly draws many thousands of us out onto the water to enjoy ourselves in our various ways.

But, to some extent this sense of freedom is an illusion. We cannot be entirely free. The natural influences of wind and tide will have their say, and then there are essential man-made rules and regulations — internationally agreed and accepted — that dictate how we must act in certain circumstances. It is the knowledge of these and other related issues that fall under the broad heading 'seamanship' and make us all seafarers, whatever reason takes us to sea. And this is not bad news. Mariners of all types have a long and admirable tradition of looking out for each other. When it comes to the crunch, you will find that the master of a cruise liner, the commercial trawlerman, the skipper in his yacht, and — as you might have guessed — the sea angler, are all very much in the same boat.

So the purpose of this book is to cover the essentials. By knowing what to do and what is expected of us, it is possible to stay safe, firstly for our own sakes and secondly to help others do the same.

Andrew Simpson

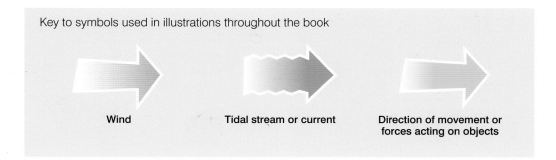

Key to symbols used in illustrations throughout the book

Wind

Tidal stream or current

Direction of movement or forces acting on objects

CONTENTS

Chapter 1

BOATS AND THEIR BITS

All-round
white ligh

Handra

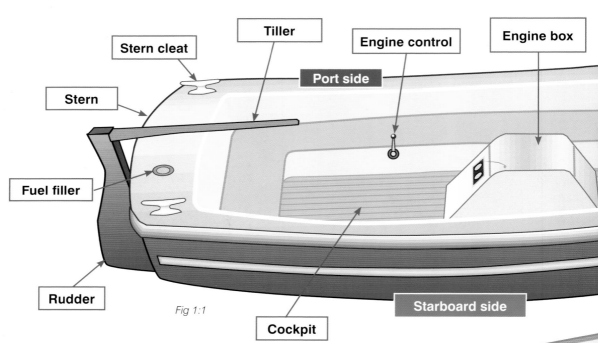

Stern cleat

Tiller

Engine control

Engine box

Port side

Stern

Fuel filler

Rudder

Fig 1:1

Cockpit

Starboard side

BOAT TYPES

Powerboat design has developed tremendously over the years. Older boats tended to be heavy and slow, while the modern trend is towards lighter and faster craft that can get us out to our favourite fishing spots as quickly as possible.

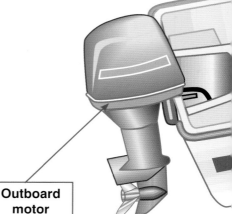

Outboard
motor

Each type has its own characteristics, offering both advantages and disadvantages.

This means there's no such thing as the perfect boat - only one that suits our purposes best. For the newcomer, the terminology can be baffling. The most basic terms are shown here.

A more comprehensive list is in the glossary starting on p109.

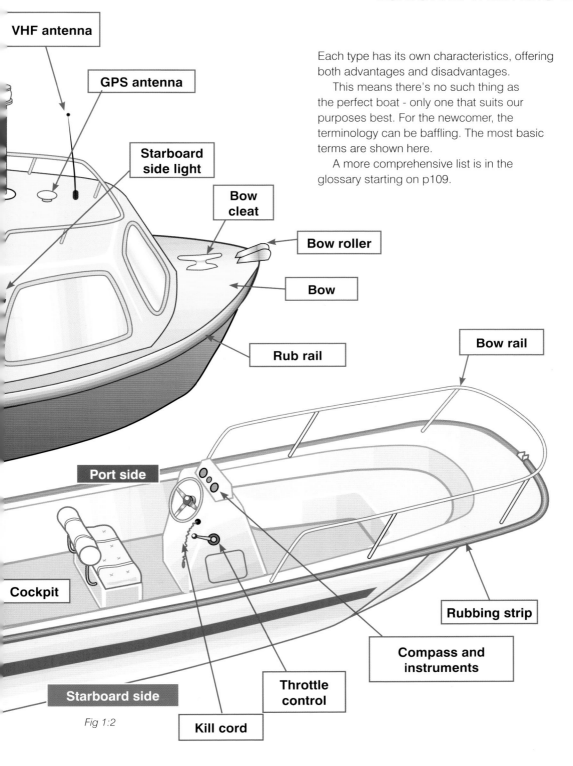

VHF antenna

GPS antenna

Starboard side light

Bow cleat

Bow roller

Bow

Rub rail

Bow rail

Port side

Cockpit

Rubbing strip

Compass and instruments

Starboard side

Throttle control

Kill cord

Fig 1:2

Heavy displacement

The word 'displacement' refers to the amount of water displaced by the hull – the weight of which is equal to the boat's weight at any moment in time. This might seem a rather roundabout way of defining how heavy a boat is but it actually works very handily, since it includes factors like the number of people on board, fuel levels and – naturally –

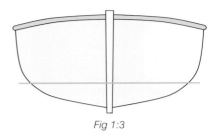

Fig 1:3

the colossal weight of your catch after a good day's fishing. Oddly, with this type the displacement has almost no affect on maximum speed, for reasons that will be explained on page 9. Heavy displacement boats have an easy, comfortable motion when under way but can roll abominably when anchored. They are usually powered by inboard engines.

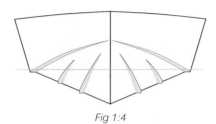

Fig 1:4

Planing hulls

Whereas heavy displacement vessels plough through the water, planing boats skim along the surface, relying on the same hydrodynamic forces that prevent water skiers from sinking. There are various hull forms but the most common for offshore use have 'V' shaped underwater sections with a number of longitudinal spray rails to help lift the boat 'onto the plane'. V-hulled boats perform poorly at low speeds but become very efficient once planing. Their veed bows allow them to slice through the waves making them particularly able performers in rough conditions. The 'fast fisher' type designs are good examples of this increasingly popular category.

Dories

The original fishing dories were flat bottomed but the modern equivalent have more complicated sections – typically being flat aft and veed towards the bow, with prominent spray rails almost at full beam that help force the waterflow under the hull and create a partial air cushion effect. They plane even more readily than V-sectioned hulls but their flatter profiles make them prone to slamming

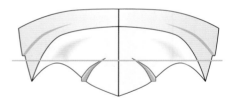

Fig 1:5

in waves. Hardly surprisingly, this makes them better suited to protected waters, where there's usually only slight wave action – though there's no reason why they shouldn't venture offshore in calm weather. Dories are nearly always powered by outboard motors.

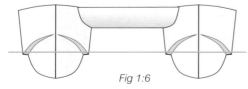

Fig 1:6

Catamarans

The word comes from the Tamil kattu-maram meaning tied wood, and describes a craft with a pair of narrow hulls joined by some form of deck structure. Since their hulls are very fine, the water doesn't have to be shouldered aside very far, so catamarans can achieve their intended design speeds with relatively less powerful engines. The twin-hulled approach inevitably brings greater than average beam, so they are exceptionally stable. At anchor they roll less than single hulled boats but their action can be rather twitchy, which some people find uncomfortable. Their wide deck usually means lots of space for anglers.

Note: There are also inflatable boats and RIBs (Rigid Inflatable Boats) but the prospect of larger fish hooks and any size gaff being waved about near to air-filled rubber tubes is somewhat risky, let's only note their existence in passing.

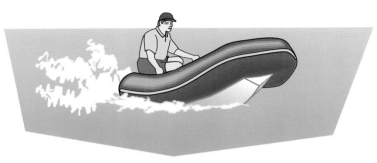

Fig 1:7

HULL SPEED

On page 10 we touched on the fact that the top speed of a displacement boat is limited by the length of its hull at the waterline. To understand why, we should imagine a boat moving forward as the throttle is progressively opened. First a small bow wave appears and another at the stern (Fig 1:8). As speed builds, a second wave appears forward and starts to move aft (Fig 1:9). Faster still and that second wave has moved all the way aft and is now reinforcing the original stern wave. The hull finds itself supported at the bow by the bow wave and at the stern by the stern wave, with a whopping great trough in between. The boat is now at its 'hull speed' – effectively as fast as she can go.

Fig 1:8 Low speed

Fig 1:9 Mid speed

What we're seeing is a relationship between forward motion and wavelength – the faster the speed, the greater will be the distance between crests, which is the reason why that second wave moved aft. If the boat attempts to go faster still, the stern wave will move away aft, clear of the transom, and the stern will sink into the trough (Fig 1:10). The boat will then literally be struggling to power uphill – clearly a hopeless task.

Fig 1:10 Maximum hull speed

A Portuguese fishing boat at hull speed. It can go no faster.

STABILITY

This is a complicated subject but the basics are very simple. Firstly, at low angles of heel a boat with a wide beam will be more stable than a narrower one. Look at the two crates shown here as **A** and **B**. Assuming they weigh the same, it's easy to appreciate why **B** – the wider one – is the more stable. Now let's compare **B** with **C**. They are both of the same size and in the same position but **C** weighs twice as much and would obviously be the most difficult to turn over – ie, the most stable.

So weight is as important as width – basically, the more you have the better. Is that the end of it? Not quite. Now look at **D** and **E**. The crates are the same size and weight but their contents are concentrated at different heights. No prizes for guessing that the one with its contents at floor level (**E**) runs less risk of being knocked over than top heavy **D**. That's simply because **E**'s Centre of Gravity (C of G) is lower.

Of course, boats float in a fluid rather than stand on solid surfaces but the principles are similar. Beamy boats with lots of weight stowed low will always be more stable than lighter, skinnier ones with their gear carried high.

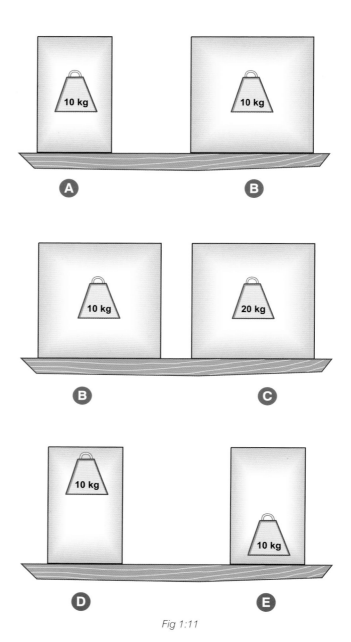

Fig 1:11

Before we leave this subject, it shouldn't be assumed that lots of stability is always a good thing. Exceptionally stable boats – the proper term is 'stiff' and the opposite is 'tender' – will snap upright with a speed that can shake your teeth loose. The ideal boat will be stiff enough to keep her feet while rolling gently so the crew doesn't suffer whiplash. To achieve the perfect compromise is one of a designer's greatest challenges.

SHIFTING WEIGHT AND FREE SURFACE EFFECT

Unlike the crates used in our crude demonstration, boats heel progressively and don't achieve their maximum stability — that's to say their maximum resistance to capsize — until heeled several degrees. The angle of maximum stability varies from design to design: as little as 10° for a catamaran, perhaps 20°–30° for a single hulled power boat and considerably more for a ballasted sailing yacht. Power boats rarely push their static stability to the limit.

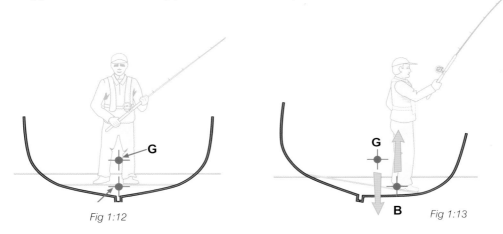

Fig 1:12   B   Fig 1:13

Let's imagine a boat at rest and floating level (Fig 1:12). The combined weight of the boat and everything it contains can be thought of as pressing downwards through its Centre of Gravity (G). This is resisted by the boat's buoyancy which pushes upwards through what's known as the Centre of Buoyancy (B). The skipper picks up his rod and moves to the gunwale to fish. His weight shifts the C of G of the whole, and the boat heels over (Fig 1:13). Note how the Centre of Buoyancy has also moved in the direction of heel so that G again exactly opposes B. The situation is once more in a state of equilibrium and will remain that way until our man changes his position.

Of course, if he was to rush repeatedly from one gunwale to the other, the boat would rock alarmingly, possibly to the point where water sloshes in and partially fills the boat (Fig 1:14). The shipped water can have disastrous effects on stability, producing an extremely dangerous phenomenon known as 'free surface effect' — the very same that caused the death of 197 people when the Herald of Free Enterprise capsized off Zeebrugge in 1987.

Once on board, the water swills from side to side, causing the boat to roll ever more wildly. Unless removed very quickly, more will be scooped up and the boat will flip or founder. To be avoided at all costs!

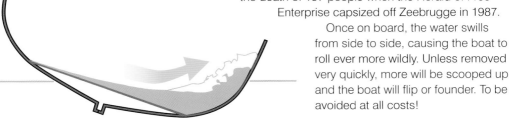

Fig 1:14

Chapter 2

ENGINES AND PROPULSION

Although their specific details may be vastly different, all marine engines work the same way and their principles are widely understood. So, we can skip through the basics in just a few words.

It involves releasing the energy contained within a combustible fuel. The fuel is first filtered to remove any debris and is then passed on to the engine. There it is combusted in cylinders (or cylinder – there may be only one) to produce what is effectively a controlled explosion. Each cylinder contains a piston that's driven down by the rapidly expanding gases, and that linear action is converted into rotary motion by a crankshaft. This is transmitted through a gearbox and onwards via some form of shaft to the propeller immersed in the water outside the hull.

By far the most popular fuels are petrol and diesel – both derived from oil – but a few engines have been converted to burn LPG (liquefied petroleum gas).

Inboard engines

The schematic (Fig 2:1) shows an 'inboard' installation. The term is self-explanatory. The fuel tank, engine – usually a diesel – gearbox and most of the shaft is inside the hull with only the propeller and the aftmost shaft bearing outside. This is the most common arrangement for heavy displacement type boats and has the virtue of simplicity and accessibility.

Incidentally, the various components that transmit the engine's power through to the water are often known collectively as the 'drive train' and, with traditional inboard installations, the parts are more or less independent of each other, meaning that you can usually work on one unit without dismantling the whole shebang. For example, if there's a problem with the gearbox you can lift that out for repair without disturbing the other components in the drive train.

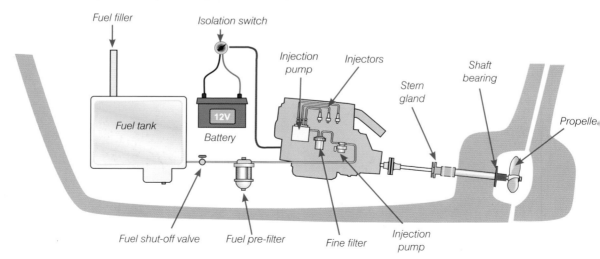

Fig 2:1

Outboard motors

There is no significance in the fact that we are now talking 'motors' rather than engines – though the distinction probably arose because early outboards were relatively feeble beasts. Not any longer. There are now a number of models exceeding 200hp (270kW) – far more powerful than many inboards.

The characteristic all outboard motors share is that the power head, gearbox and prop are combined in a single assembly – usually clad in a sleek casing. The smallest ones also have built-in fuel tanks. This integrated approach makes them exceptionally easy to fit. You simply mount them on the stern, connect up the controls, fuel supply and electrics (as appropriate) and you're in business. Smaller outboards are also portable. You can take them home in the back of your car at the end of your day's fishing.

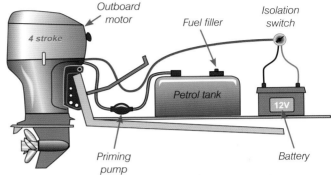

Outboard motor / Fuel filler / Isolation switch / 4 stroke / Petrol tank / 12V / Priming pump / Battery

Outboard motors do more then just propel the boat – they steer it as well. This is achieved by swivelling the whole unit so the thrust from the prop pushes the stern to one side or the other. Most can also be tilted, either to influence the trim of the boat or to stow the outboard with the prop clear of the water.

Although there are a few diesel outboards to be found, the overwhelming majority are petrol fuelled.

Inboard/outboards

This hybrid arrangement combines inboard engines with outboard drive legs – the latter often called 'stern drives' or 'outdrives'. Larger and more powerful engines (up to about 400hp (538kW)) can be fitted and, because these are carried low in the boat, their weight improves rather than reduces stability. Stern drives can be steered and tilted in much the same way as outboards. The engines can be either diesel or petrol.

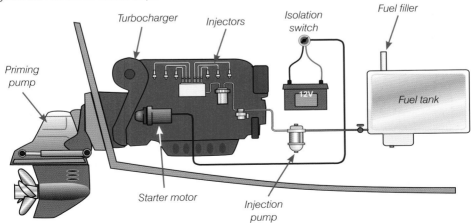

Priming pump / Turbocharger / Injectors / Isolation switch / Fuel filler / 12V / Fuel tank / Starter motor / Injection pump

MATCHING THE MACHINERY

It's essential that the boat and the various components in the drive train are well matched to your intended usage. This means there has to be the right engine for the boat and the right prop for the engine. Judging this isn't as easy as it sounds and almost always involves making compromises, since any combination will only operate at its peak efficiency over a narrow range of conditions. Yet we often expect too much. For instance, we might have a very powerful engine in a high speed boat and ask it to troll at just 3 knots for several hours when it would be much happier roaring along at 30. Not only will the engine be running inefficiently but it might actually be suffering damage. In those circumstances a slower boat with a smaller engine might have been the better choice.

Unfortunately, this is too big a subject to explore in depth here. Luckily, there's plenty of information out there to refer to.

DIAMETER, PITCH AND SLIP

Propellers are classified by their diameter, pitch and direction of rotation. The first is, of course, the diameter of the circle swept by the blades, and rotation is the direction the upper blades move if viewed from astern. For example, if seen to turn clockwise, the upper blades will move to starboard and you have a 'right handed' prop. If they turn the other way – ie, anticlockwise – the prop is left handed.

Pitch is the least easy to understand. It is best thought of as the distance a propeller would screw itself forward if it was to make one revolution in an unyielding material. Sadly, water isn't unyielding so this is a largely theoretical concept. In reality, the prop will never 'advance' 100% of its pitch, and that shortfall between advance and pitch is called 'slip' – and there can be a lot of it in headwinds or, perhaps, with a fouled or heavily laden boat. Expressed as a percentage of pitch, slip can easily be as much as 50%.

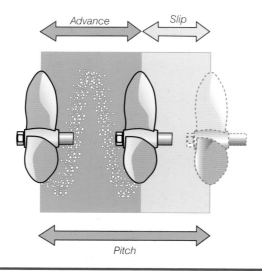

Advance *Slip*

Pitch

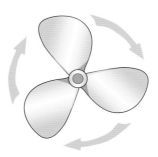

A right handed prop. Viewed from the stern the blades when at the top turn to the right.

BEARINGS AND STERN GLANDS

With outboards and stern drives, you can usually select which pitch of propeller suits your intentions best, but the units as a whole come already assembled so there are few other options. That's not the case with conventional inboard installations which are put together by the boat builder pretty much as he sees fit. The engine comes from one supplier, the shaft from another, the bearings ditto and so on. Hardly surprisingly, there are various ways of going about the job, some better than others.

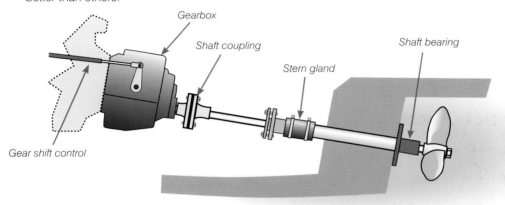

Unlike outboards and stern drives, conventional prop shafts exit the boat beneath the waterline. This creates a point of acute vulnerability that must be dealt with – quite a thorny problem since the hole must be kept watertight while allowing the shaft to rotate within it. Luckily, propeller driven vessels have been with us for over 150 years so there's been plenty of time to come up with engineering solutions.

Early glands were known as 'stuffing boxes' – and there are still thousands of them in service. They contain a packing material (usually made of flax) which is lightly compressed around the shaft to form a seal. The word 'lightly' is important here, for if the packing material bears too hard against the shaft, the friction causes it to overheat and there will be excessive wear to the shaft. Indeed, stuffing boxes are intended to leak a little – two or three drips a minute is ideal – and should be adjusted periodically to keep them functioning properly.

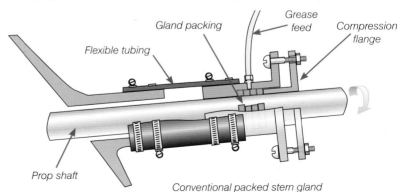

Conventional packed stern gland

Over the last decade or so there has been a rush of development. Modern stern glands need no adjustment and shouldn't leak at all. The most popular types fall into two categories – 'lip seals' and 'face seals', both offered by various manufacturers.

Lip seals:

These work in a similar way to the oil seals in your engine. A thin rubber lip (or lips, there could be more than one) presses against the shaft in such a manner that the water pressure holds the two close together. Because the contact area is small, there's hardly any friction. Lip seals are essentially water lubricated but some types need an occasional squirt of grease to help them along.

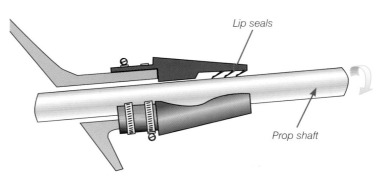

Lip seals

Prop shaft

Lip seal type stern gland

Face seals:

These employ an entirely different principle. The seal is made in two parts. One part is a polished stainless steel ring that's clamped to the shaft and rotates with it. The second comprises another ring – this time of graphite – which is held pressed against the first ring by a rubber bellows clamped to the protruding end of the stern tube. This, of course, remains static.

The faces of the two rings slide one against the other with very little friction. Face seals are always water lubricated.

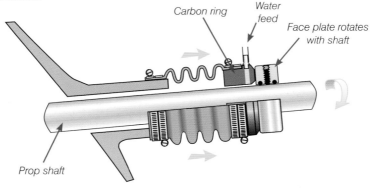

Carbon ring   Water feed   Face plate rotates with shaft

Prop shaft

With either type of seal it's important to acquaint yourself with what maintenance they need to keep them healthy. Because they don't demand much attention it's all too easy to neglect them. They will last for years if treated properly.

STEERING

How a boat is steered depends on the way it's propelled. Those with outboards or stern drives steer with their drive units, while more traditional craft – that's to say those with fixed shafts and props – must rely on rudders. Although the distinctions between them might at first seem unimportant, it makes a significant difference to their handling techniques – a subject we shall be dealing with later in this chapter.

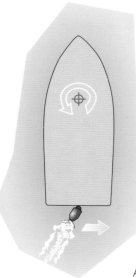

Steering with prop thrust

Basically, if the thrust is dead astern, the boat will move forward in a straight line. If the thrust is directed, say, towards the starboard side, the stern will be pushed to port and the boat will swing to starboard. Naturally, the opposite would be true if you turned the helm the other way.

An important point to remember is that the ability to steer is entirely dependent on the thrust. As soon as you put the engine in neutral you lose that control. Both outboard motors and stern drives share this characteristic and, since outboards are likely to be the commoner of the two on angling boats, from henceforth we shall lump them both together under the word 'outboard'.

Steering with a rudder

The usual arrangement is to have the prop immediately forward of the rudder so that turning the blade can deflect the prop's thrust – also called prop-wash – from side to side. In some ways this achieves the same result as the previous method but there's one crucial difference. Although the prop-wash makes the actions of the rudder more powerful, it isn't absolutely essential.

So long as the boat continues to move through the water there will be waterflow over the rudder blade and you will have some steerage, regardless of whether the prop is turning or not. Unfortunately, some motorboat rudders can be very small – particularly those on high speed planing craft. Without the prop-wash these are virtually useless. However, most angling boats are designed to operate at low speeds, so have sensibly sized rudders – something this book takes for granted in all the situations described.

Rudder steered boats don't steer particularly well astern. This is because the prop-wash is no longer flowing over the surface of the rudder, which must then rely on whatever waterflow there is.

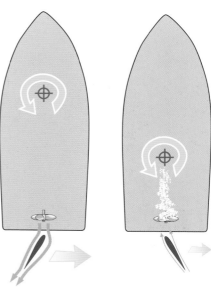

The steering controls

The crew's input into the steering process is via a tiller or wheel. Tillers are simple and reliable devices, since they are nothing more than long handles that you move from side to side to turn the rudder or outboard. But they come with limitations: firstly, they confine helmsmen to the sterns of their boats and, secondly, there are practical size limits. Wheels, on the other hand, may be sited anywhere and can incorporate some form of gearing or engine-driven servo assistance that allows you to control even the largest rudder or motor.

The linkage between the wheel and stern gear comes in various forms: wires, chains, push rods, torque tubes, hydraulics – even electronic in swankier boats. There isn't room to review all the options here, but it generally pays to keep everything as simple as possible and remember that you might have to improvise a repair when far from land.

GEAR SHIFTS AND THROTTLES

There are also various types of engine controls. The most direct arrangement could be a twist grip on an outboard motor or a lever poking up straight from the gearbox, but most engine controls are mounted remotely. And, again there's a choice of linkage. By far the most common systems have a pair of 'Bowden' cables. These are similar to bicycle brake cables, with an inner wire running inside a tubular conduit. However, unlike brake cables whose inner wire can only pull, the Bowden type can both pull and push. You need one cable for the gears and another for the throttle – usually operated by a single lever mechanical control box fitted within reach of the steering position.

Operation is simple. With the lever in the middle (usually upright) position, the gearbox is in neutral and the engine ticking over. When you move the lever forward, the control's first action is to engage forward gear. Further movement progressively increases the revs, with the lever now effectively acting as a throttle. Going astern works in the same way but, of course, in this case the control lever is moved sternwards. There's invariably a provision (often a button) which allows you to rev the engine without engaging a gear – useful if, for instance, you want to run the engine to charge the batteries.

Chapter 3

PLANNING AND SAFETY

No boat should put to sea without first checking that it's fit to do so. Yet the rescue services report that an astonishing number of them find themselves in trouble because something simple has been overlooked.

Anglers are naturally patient individuals – their sport demands it! – so are unlikely to begrudge a few minutes making sure their boat is shipshape before they cast off the mooring lines and head for their favourite fishing ground.

Things to check before you even start the engine are:

■ Do you have enough fuel? Although this seems an obvious point, every year sees scores of boats towed in with dry tanks. And remember that a centimetre or two in the bottom might seem enough until the boat starts to roll. Then the fuel sloshes from side to side and air is drawn into the system.

■ Check fuel filters for debris or water. How to deal with any problems is covered in Chapter 13.

■ Check the engine's lubricating oil, gearbox oil, and coolant water levels (Fig 3:1).

■ All belts should be in good condition and correctly tensioned (Fig 3:2).

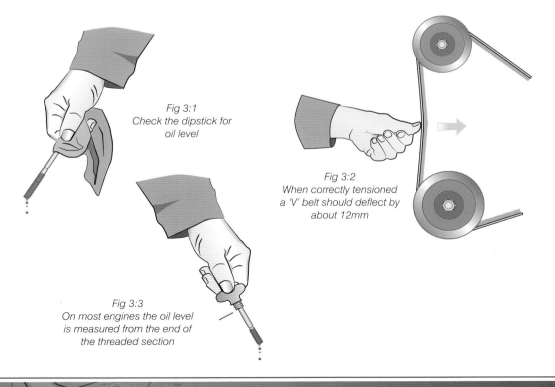

Fig 3:1
Check the dipstick for
oil level

Fig 3:2
When correctly tensioned
a 'V' belt should deflect by
about 12mm

Fig 3:3
On most engines the oil level
is measured from the end of
the threaded section

- Make sure the seawater cooling inlet strainer is free of debris. If the strainer is below the waterline, this will mean first closing the seacock. Take care to open the seacock again before starting the engine.

- With outboard motors, ensure the air vent on the tank is open.

- Finally, have a general look around the engine and transmission looking for leaks, loose electrical connections or anything else amiss.

Before you fire up the engine, take a glance over the stern to make sure there's nothing there that might foul the prop. Once started, check that a healthy flow of cooling water is being expelled with the exhaust. Then allow the engine to idle for a few minutes to come up to its normal operating temperature. A great deal of internal wear can occur if a cold engine is put under load too quickly.

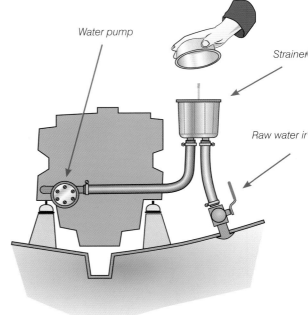

Water pump

Strainer

Raw water in

If the strainer is fitted above the waterline the lid can be removed with the boat afloat.

Other important checks

- Notify a contact ashore of your departure: the time you intend leaving, where you intend fishing, and when you expect to expect to return.

- Obtain the latest weather report.

- Make sure all the safety gear is on board. A typical list is detailed in the panel opposite and will be discussed more fully in Chapter 12.

- Test the steering. Turn it from lock to lock. It should operate smoothly, without any obvious twitches of abnormal resistance that might indicate a frayed wire or other malfunctioning component.

- Turn batteries on.

- The amount of electrical equipment carried varies greatly from boat to boat. Depending on your own inventory, you should test bilge pumps, VHF, GPS (or chartplotter), trim tabs, outdrive leg tilt mechanism and navigation lights.

BASIC SAFETY GEAR

- Anchor and warp
- Kill cord and spare
- Bilge pump and/or bailer
- Engine spares and tools
- Radar reflector
- Compass
- VHF radio (fixed or hand-held)
- Flares
- Horn

- Tide tables
- Charts
- Relevant shapes (i.e. anchor ball)
- Lifejackets for all on board and spare canisters
- Fire extinguisher(s)
- Fire blanket
- First Aid kit
- Heaving line

- Auxiliary outboard or paddles
- Fenders and mooring lines
- Navigation lights
- Mobile phone in waterproof jacket
- Food and water
- Warm clothing
- Tools, including serrated knife

Additionally, a boat going further offshore might also carry:

- GPS (fixed or hand-held) or chart plotter
- Hand bearing compass
- Depth sounder
- Radar
- Lifebuoy and danbuoy
- Navtex receiver (for weather reports)
- EPIRB
- Liferaft

Brief the crew

Once you have owned a boat for a while, you get to know it intimately. You know what gear is on board, where it's stowed and what sort of condition it's in. For instance, there's a rather dodgy fire extinguisher stowed in a cockpit locker but you are also aware that there's a newer and much larger one clipped to the wheelhouse bulkhead.

Faced with a fire you would undoubtedly ignore the first and reach for the second. Likewise, that tatty old rope you keep coiled up in the forepeak. Is that the one you would choose if about to be taken in tow? Certainly not if there's a better one you have stowed elsewhere.

But, of course, you're the skipper and understand the options. But what about others that might be aboard? What decisions might they make in an emergency if you were suddenly put out of action?

It can't be overemphasised how important it is to share vital information with everybody else. It need only take a few minutes and might even seem a little embarrassing, but such knowledge could easily prevent a simple incident becoming a full-blown tragedy.

Your briefing should include at least:

■ Starting and stopping the engine, including use of kill cord if one is fitted.

■ Basic boat handling – particularly so they can turn back for you if you are the MOB (Man Overboard).

■ Anchoring – how and in what circumstances.

■ How to operate the bilge pumps, both manual and electric.

■ Location of the first aid kit.

■ Location and use of lifejackets – including how to adjust them for size. It's a good idea to allocate one to each crew and make sure they all fit.

■ Location and use of flares.

■ Operating the VHF to send a Mayday message.

Of course, the main responsibility for holding such briefings rests with the skipper, but remember that it's the safety of everybody aboard that's at stake. If the skipper doesn't volunteer the information, the others should ask him. And, if he doesn't explain everything satisfactorily, *they should ask him again.*

Chapter 4

BOAT HANDLING

OF WIND AND WATER

Before we cast off and go fishing, it might help to think about the nature of the environment we're entering and see how dissimilar it is to the landlubberly world we're familiar with. Compare driving a car to manoeuvring a boat. Ashore, the road is stationary beneath the car's wheels. There may be some buffeting from strong winds but the driver can expect his vehicle to remain steadily on track, following the path he has chosen for it.

The boat on the other hand is carried on a moving platform of water that can flow in any direction, depending on currents, tides and other factors. We'll call them all 'streams' unless the type of stream makes a difference. Then there's the effect of the wind. A boat's grip on the water is much less than that of tyres on tarmac, so even a modest breeze can blow it off course.

This may all sound like bad news – and it has to be admitted that it can cause problems – but, once you understand the principles, you can put them to good use. Indeed, you can make boats perform manoeuvres that cars are incapable of. For instance, boats can move directly sideways, perhaps to slot into a gap only inches longer than themselves. This trick is known as 'ferry gliding' – a technique employed by small ferries and other craft since the earliest days of power.

Let's see how it's done.

Ferry gliding

Stand on a busy quayside and watch the tripper boats enter and leave. One boat might be waiting a few metres off, apparently motionless, while another is busy alongside pulling up its gangplank and casting off its mooring lines. Soon the second boat leaves and, without fuss, the waiting one slides into the now vacant berth to take its place.

Now, you might think that the waiting boat was just adrift with its engine in neutral, but that could not be so. A strong tidal stream runs along the quay and would have swept it away. What it was actually doing was pointing its bow exactly into the stream and maintaining just enough forward power to overcome it – 'stemming the tide' as it's called. If, say, the stream was running at two knots, the boat would have to maintain two knots through the water to remain stationary. And neither was the helmsman sitting back having a cuppa with his feet up because that phrase 'exactly into the tide' is extremely important in keeping that boat in position. If the boat were allowed to skew a little, say, to port, the boat would crab sideways in that direction, and vice-versa. Done deliberately, that

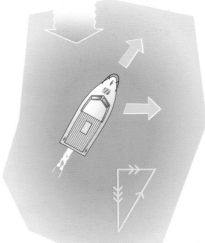

Fig 4:1 The combined forces of the stream and the boat's course and speed through the water result in a sideways movement

crabbing action is the secret of ferry gliding and lies at the base of so many useful manoeuvres. In such circumstances the tide is our friend not our enemy.

Back to basics

It might seem odd to start a chapter on boat handling with such a manoeuvre, but ferry gliding demonstrates how simple it is to employ both the forces of nature (the stream) and those under our control (power and steering) to work to our advantage. All it takes is a little understanding to make what might seem impossible actually very easy.

Wind and stream are the two natural forces that affect us the most. Planing boats have very little grip on the water and can be relatively easily blown about by the wind – especially those with high superstructures like motor cruisers. Displacement boats sit much deeper and are more affected by the stream.

Every skipper should be aware of what's happening around him at all times. That's important enough in open water but becomes absolutely vital in close quarters. If, for instance, our ferry skipper had attempted a downstream approach in the same circumstances, the results would certainly have been embarrassing and probably very expensive.

And there are lots of clues to tell us what's going on:

Wind

- Flags waving in the breeze.
- Drift of any nearby smoke.
- The wind effect on the surface of the water.
- Or you can improvise a simple wind indicator by tying a short length of light fishing line to some exposed part of the boat.

> **BEWARE:** the movement of low clouds may give you a general indication of wind direction but this may not be the same as at sea level.

Stream

- Observe boats at anchor nearby. Unless the wind is exceptionally strong, they will lie with their bows pointing into the stream. Sailing yachts with their deep keels are particularly reliable.
- Water flowing past fixed objects such as navigational marks or buoys.
- Only when alongside: tight mooring lines and debris floating by are both good indicators.

The experienced skipper notices these things almost subconsciously, keeping himself constantly aware of any shifts. But the novice is often so overwhelmed with information that he may not take it all in. In open waters this may not matter much, but when manoeuvring in close quarters it's of huge importance.

A good way to practise is by picking up a mooring buoy – preferably one with lots of space around it so if things go wrong no harm will be done. So … having selected your buoy, what then?

- First and foremost, you must decide which way the stream is flowing. Look at other boats moored nearby and – of course – observe how the stream flows around the buoy itself. Remember that the effects can be extremely localised. Focus on your immediate vicinity.

- You are going to approach the buoy from dead downstream. This is one of the golden rules of boat handling. That way the stream will act as a natural brake and you can move your boat sideways if you need to using the ferry gliding technique described on page 25.

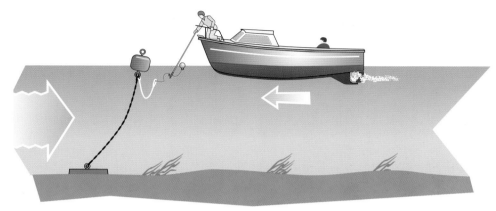

Fig 4:2

■ Having positioned your boat downstream, you simply head towards the buoy, using the throttle to control your approach speed. Side to side positioning is controlled by the steering. With a bit of practice you will find that you can take your boat right up to the buoy and hold it there stationary while making fast. And, of course, if things go wrong you can just pull back the throttle and allow the stream to carry you safely back to where you can try again (Fig 4:2).

> **REMEMBER!** When motoring with the stream your speed over the ground will be your speed through the water plus that of the stream. When motoring against the stream your speed over the ground is your speed through the water minus that of the stream.

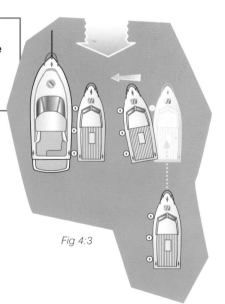

Mastering the principles of ferry gliding allows you to perform a number of useful manoeuvres in a calm and risk free manner. A good example is coming alongside an anchored boat. Instead of sweeping in as you might bring your car in towards a parking space, you should bring your boat to a position parallel to the other boat and then gently ferry glide alongside (Fig 4:3).

Fig 4:3

TIP A good way to temporarily secure to a mooring buoy is to lasso it with a bight (loop) of rope. Make both ends fast to the boat and then drop the loop over the buoy.

TURNING TECHNIQUES

Back on page 19 we learned that outboards and outdrives have different steering characteristics to the more traditional fixed prop and rudder types, namely…

Outboards and outdrives can only steer the boat when the propeller is turning because they rely solely on the thrust. Try and remember the phrase 'steer before gear' meaning that you should turn the drive leg to where you want it before you open the throttle.

Conventional rudders will continue to steer so long as there's waterflow over their blades (it's called 'steerageway') whether the prop is turning or not. However, rudders are much more efficient when that waterflow is boosted by prop thrust.

Before we discuss how to deal with these differences, let's expand briefly on propellers. As well as the thrust that propels a boat either forward or sternwards, there's another less obvious action at work. This is known as 'prop-walk' – a sort of paddle-wheel effect that introduces a small amount of sideways propulsion, particularly when going astern. We can use this to advantage when turning our boats.

> **REMEMBER: A right-handed prop will kick to port when going astern. A left-handed prop will kick to starboard.**

Single screw and rudder

This type relies heavily on prop-walk. First, you should…

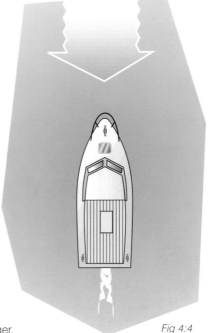

■ Establish which way the stern will kick when going astern. If you already know whether the prop is left or right handed, you can work it out. If not, try looking into the bilge to see which way the shaft is rotating or simply experiment in advance by putting the rudder amidships and giving a quick burst astern. The wash should emerge predominantly from one side or the other and the stern will kick in the opposite direction (Fig 4:4).

■ Check the direction of wind and stream. It is always better to turn the boat into the wind and stream to avoid being swept down. If their directions conflict, prop and rudder boats should pay more attention to the stream.

Right, you are ready to start. Go easy on the throttle because too much speed makes the turning circle larger. Let's assume our boat has a right handed prop which means the stern will kick to port in reverse.

Fig 4:4

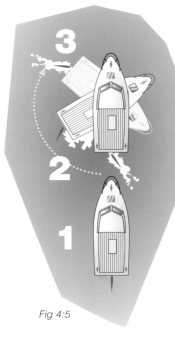

1 **Approaching slowly, position your boat in the centre of the space.**

2 **Put the rudder hard over so the boat will turn to starboard. At the same time give a quick burst ahead – no more than a couple of seconds – before returning to neutral. The rudder will deflect the thrust and the stern will be pushed to port. The boat will move only a short distance forward.**

3 **Leave the rudder where it is and give a similar short burst astern. The rudder is useless with so little steerageway, so it's now the turn of the prop-walk which kicks the stern further to port.**

You can repeat this sequence until the bow has swung round enough to return the way you came. Engage forward gear and away you go.

Fig 4:5

Outboard motors or outdrives

Prop-walk is both less powerful and less useful with this type of boat. However, the steerable thrust more than compensates – though you will have to work harder!

1 **As before, approach slowly and position your boat in the centre of the space.**

2 **Turn the wheel hard over to port then – and only then! – give a quick burst ahead before returning to neutral.**

3 **Now turn the wheel hard over to starboard. A quick burst astern and the angled reverse thrust pulls the stern round to port.**

Again, repeat the sequence until you can steer safely out.

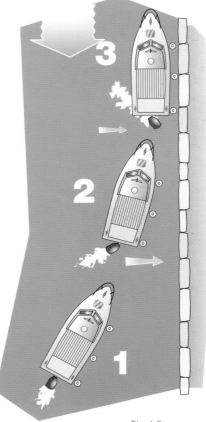

Fig 4:6

BERTHING ALONGSIDE

The ferry gliding described on page 23 is an excellent method of slotting your boat into a small gap but, of course, berthing isn't always that demanding. On many occasions there's plenty of space and you can simply steer your boat alongside.

But that doesn't mean you can forget wind and stream. As always, take advantage of their slowing effect by heading into them whenever possible.

Single prop and rudder (Fig 4:7)

1 Approach at an angle of about 30° to the berth and at slow speed – perhaps even with the engine in neutral for the last few metres.

2 With the bow about a metre away from the quay, put the helm hard over and give a quick burst of forward power. This will kick the stern in with almost no acceleration in your speed.

3 Finally, stop the boat completely with a burst astern – even more effective if the prop-walk helps to pin you alongside.

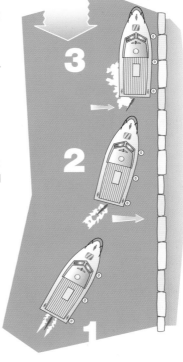

Fig 4:7

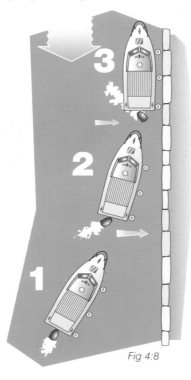

Fig 4:8

Steerable drive boats (Fig 4:8)

1 Make your approach as before, shifting in and out of forward gear to keep the speed down.

2 Again, with the bow about a metre from touching, steer away from the quay and give a short burst ahead.

3 To stop the boat and pull the stern in further, steer hard over the other way and give an equally short burst astern.

LEARNING THE ROPES

Of course, having made it alongside, you will have to tie up your boat to prevent it drifting away. It usually takes four separate ropes – more usually called lines – to secure a boat to a quayside or pontoon. And the naming of these is fraught with confusion. For instance a 'bow line' could be a rope from the bow whereas a 'bowline' (pronounced 'bowlin') is a type of knot. And there are those would claim that a 'back spring' (and here I'm ignoring anything to do with gymnastics) would be a rope leading forward from the stern to a cleat on the dock, while others would call the same a 'fore spring' because – they would argue – it leads forward.

So, for the sake of all our sanities, let's step back from the squabbling and adopt the following terms:

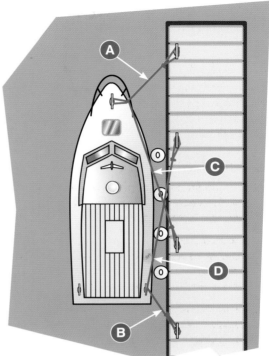

Fig 4:9

- **Bow line (A)** a line leading a little way forward from the bow to the shore or pontoon. On short pontoons, it may be impossible to take the bow line forward, so a shorter bow line is rigged pretty much at 90°, in which case it should more correctly be called a 'breast rope'. Either way, their purpose is to hold the bow securely in against its fenders.

- **Stern line (B)** a line leading some way aft from the stern and serving much the same purpose as the bow line. Again, in cramped circumstances it may have to be rigged as a breast rope.

- **Bow spring (C)** a line led as far aft as is practical from the bow. Its job is to prevent the boat from surging forward.

- **Stern spring (D)** the mirror image of the above – a line from the stern secured to the dock as far forward as is practical. Stern springs prevent the boat surging aft.

ROPES TO THE RESCUE

You may wonder why we are suddenly referring to mooring lines in a chapter on boat handling. This is because they can be much more than just simple tethers. There are many instances when an intelligent use of lines can overcome otherwise difficult circumstances.

Have another look at the drawings Fig 4:7 and Fig 4:8. You will see that the wind is assisting our two skippers by blowing their boats against the quay – what's known as an 'onshore wind'. Think how tricky it would be if faced with the opposite – a brisk 'offshore wind'. With your boat laid alongside you would have to get some lines ashore pretty smartly to avoid being blown away. Not always easy to do when alone or shorthanded.

Fortunately, a single line will do the trick.

Get your bow line on first

- Boats with steerable drives should secure their bows first (Fig 4:10). This doesn't mean someone has to leap across the gap from the bow. A 'bight' (loop) can often be dropped over cleat from the widest point of the hull, before allowing the boat to drop back on the stream.

- Next, turn the wheel towards the quay and put the engine astern. This will pull the stern around until it's neatly alongside. Once your other lines are secured, you can select neutral and shut down the engine.

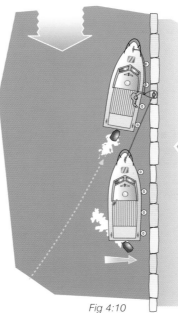

Fig 4:10

Midships spring

Of course, this technique won't work with rudder steered boats but there's an equally effective alternative that will.

- Rig a short spring from a cleat at about mid-length (Fig 4:11). At a pinch you could use a bow spring, but midships is much better. Tie a fair sized eye in the free end and drop it over a cleat when you come alongside.

- Put the rudder hard over as if steering away from the berth and engage forward gear. The boat will move ahead until checked by the spring, and the stern will be driven in towards the quay. So long as the rudder stays hard over, it will stay there comfortably while you get your other lines ashore. If the wind threatens to blow you off, simply whack on more throttle.

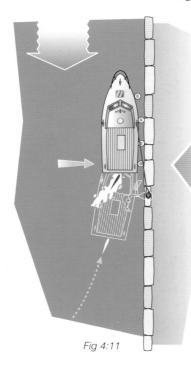

Fig 4:11

LEAVING THE BERTH

The effects of onshore or offshore winds are reversed when you want to depart. With the wind blowing offshore you can often simply cast off and let the wind carry you clear. But with the wind pinning you against a quay or pontoon it can be a good deal trickier.

Luckily, it just so happens that variations on the previous two techniques employed to bring us alongside will also serve when we want to depart.

Steerable drives

- This couldn't be easier. First rig a 'slip line' by securing a rope to the bow, taking it round the shore cleat or bollard, and bringing the other end back on board where it too is temporarily secured (Fig 4:12). Let go all other mooring lines.

- Turn the wheel as if steering away from the quay and put the engine astern. The stern will swing out to the point where you can release the slip line and back out into clear water.

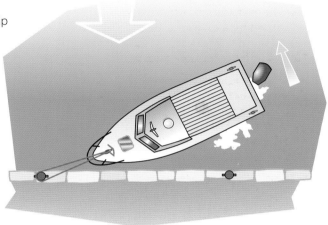

Fig 4:12

Single prop and rudder

- This manoeuvre is called 'springing off'. It's a little more complicated. Rig either a bow or stern spring as a slip line and, again, let go the other lines.

- If using a stern spring you should engage astern gear; if springing from the bow you will use forward gear (Fig 4:13). You should apply just enough power to rotate the boat until you are able to slip the spring and motor clear. Whichever way you depart, a strategically placed fender will be necessary to protect the hull.

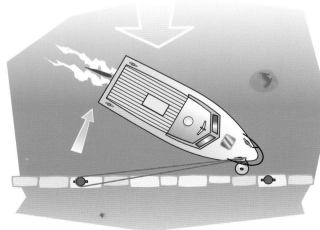

Fig 4:13

ANCHORING

Sea anglers tend to spend a lot of time at anchor – and not always in ideal situations. Fishing for bass, for instance, is often done when and where the tides are at their strongest. Few other recreational boaters would anchor in such circumstances.

The equipment you use is known collectively as 'ground tackle' and comprises the anchor itself and the 'rode' – the cable that connects the anchor to the boat. There are many different types of anchors and a selection of the most common are shown below. Each manufacturer has a tendency to claim that their own product is superior, but the truth is that all anchors hold better in some seabeds than others. An anchor that might hold well in soft mud might be less secure in gravel and so on. However, most modern anchors are pretty good all-rounders and will perform tolerably well in most conditions. The traditional 'fisherman' type anchor is excellent on rock and heavy weed and should not be dismissed on account of its antiquity.

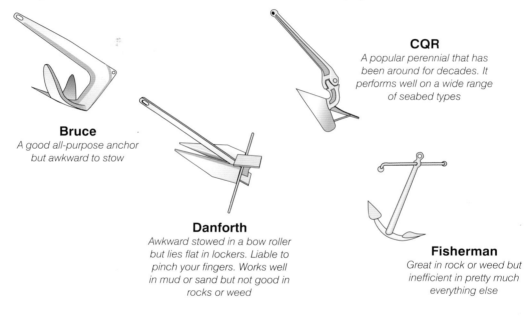

CQR
A popular perennial that has been around for decades. It performs well on a wide range of seabed types

Bruce
A good all-purpose anchor but awkward to stow

Danforth
Awkward stowed in a bow roller but lies flat in lockers. Liable to pinch your fingers. Works well in mud or sand but not good in rocks or weed

Fisherman
Great in rock or weed but inefficient in pretty much everything else

Of equal importance to the anchor is the rode. This can be of chain, rope or a combination of both. Chain is the by far the best choice but can be impracticable on smaller boats. An all-rope rode is vulnerable to abrasion, which leaves a mix of chain and rope as a good compromise. In practice this usually means 5m or so of chain and the rest of nylon rope. Never use polypropylene as it floats and, at slack water, could rise to the surface and foul both your prop and your fishing lines.

Anchors are designed to work best when the pull on them is as near horizontal as possible. This is one reason why the short length of chain is so important. Its weight holds the shank of the anchor down. It's also vital that you let out plenty of rode. Five times the depth of water is about right. Any shorter and the pull from the rode will be more upwards than horizontal and the anchor could be pulled out – especially if the boat is snatching in the waves.

Dropping anchor

- Rather like picking up a mooring buoy, make your approach into the dominant flow – stream or wind, most likely the former in tidal waters.

- Lower the anchor smoothly and allow the boat to be carried back, paying out the rode as you go. Don't just toss it over the side in a big tangle. If the rode fouls the anchor it may not hold. If there is no stream or wind you should motor astern.

- With the rode secured, give the engine a burst astern to dig the anchor in. If it's holding properly, the rode should be seen stretching forward, bar taut. Time to start fishing.

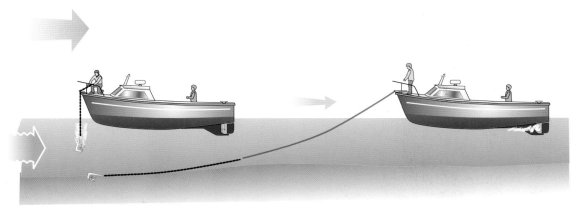

Sheer ingenuity

There is often good fishing to be had in deep navigation channels, such as the entrance to harbours. However, these channels are often dredged and may be too deep to anchor comfortably or the bottom may be churned up and insecure.

A good trick is to anchor in the adjacent shallows and then put the helm over so the tidal stream carries you out over the deeper water. Then, if a ship comes along you need only put the helm amidships and your boat will glide back out of the way. Don't forget to readjust the helm when the tide turns, otherwise you may find yourself aground.

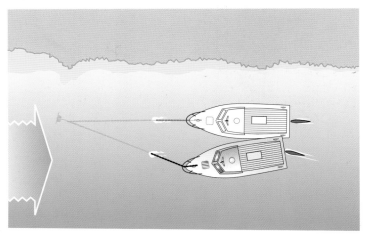

Dragging

Since anglers spend most of their time on deck, this is rarely a serious issue but it's still not the sort of problem you would want to go unnoticed. When inshore, the most convenient check is to line up a couple of features ashore – known as a 'transit'. Ideally, your transit should be more or less abeam and comprise a close object and a distant one. So long as they remain in line, you know your position isn't changing.

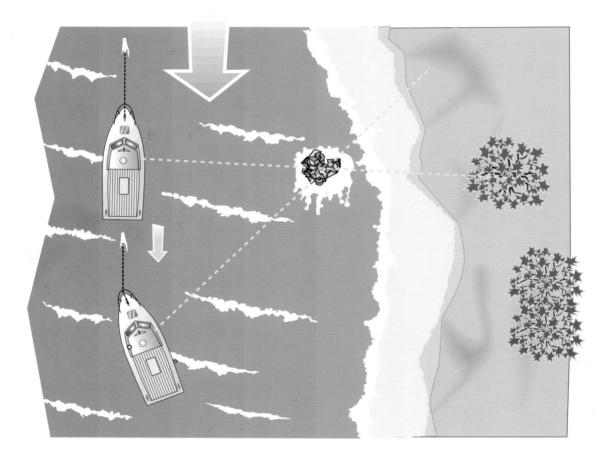

Another sign that you might be dragging is if the boat fails to lie true to the wind or stream. Anchors often drag in a series of jerks – pulling free then catching, and so on. In those circumstances the bow will tend to fall away then suddenly straighten. The first remedy is to let out more rode. If that doesn't work there is a good chance you have a bunch of weed around the anchor, in which case there is no alternative but to pull it up and clear it before re-anchoring.

Chapter 5

ROPEWORK

Although the materials are very different, ropes and the ways we use them would have been familiar to prehistoric man. In fact the switch from natural fibres is a surprisingly recent development, with sisal, manila and cotton giving way to modern synthetics only during the last half of the 20th century.

Synthetic ropes are described by their construction and material, with the last being the most important. Constructional options divide between the traditional and most easily recognisable 3-strand and various types of braided or plaited ropes. 3-strand is generally the least expensive and is by far the easiest to splice (see page 39).

There are some very exotic modern fibres around, but only three that really interest us:

Nylon

This is a material all anglers will be familiar with, since in its monofilament form it represents by far the most common type of fishing line. It's strong and stretchy – exactly what you want to absorb shock loads. And the same qualities that allow it to withstand the strike of a big fish also make it ideal for anchor warps and mooring lines.

Nylon has good resistance both to abrasion and attack by UV light. Unfortunately, it is slightly absorbent and becomes stiffer when wet. Over a period of time this process draws impurities into the fibres and the rope can become permanently stiff and awkward to handle.

Polyester

Having about the same strength but much less stretch than nylon, polyester is a deservedly popular rope for general usage. Because it remains soft and flexible even when wet, many skippers prefer it for their mooring lines, despite its lack of elasticity. Polyester stands up to UV light pretty well and is resistant to flexural fatigue. An excellent all-round performer.

Polypropylene

The main claim to fame of this lightweight fibre is that it floats. It has much the same stretch characteristics as polyester but is only about 65% as strong. It's also more susceptible to UV degradation than the other two.

Nevertheless, it has its merits. Its natural buoyancy makes it the obvious choice for such things as lifebuoy tethers and heaving lines (see page 44) and it's also relatively inexpensive.

KNOTS

It will come as no surprise to learn that knots are as important to mariners as they are to anglers. However, there is one important difference. Whereas fishing knots are designed to lock solid once tied, and must be cut free to release them, those used on boats must be both secure in use and easy to untie.

There are literally hundreds of different sailors' knots but only a few that are used regularly. If you can tie those shown here you will not go far wrong. RYA Pocket Book of Boating Knots, order code G60, is a good guide.

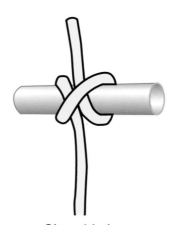

Bowline
Pronounced 'bow-lin' with the bow as in bow and arrow. This is probably the most useful knot of all. It's most commonly used to form loops – such as in the ends of mooring lines. Easy to undo if made properly.

Clove hitch
Useful for tasks like securing the end of a dinghy painter to a rail. Note how the ends of the rope emerge from the knot pointing in opposite directions as shown here. If they point the same way you probably have a 'cow hitch' which is not so secure.

Reef knot
Tied just like your shoelaces should be, but without developing the fancy loops. The tying method is often described as 'right over left and under, then left over right and under'. Make sure you don't tie a 'granny knot' which is similar but doesn't lie flat.

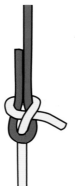

Sheet bend
An excellent way of tying the ends of two ropes together. Never use a reef knot for this purpose. It can invert and pull free.

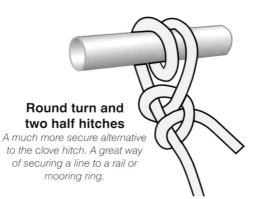

Round turn and two half hitches
A much more secure alternative to the clove hitch. A great way of securing a line to a rail or mooring ring.

WHIPPINGS

Called rather unkindly the 'butane whipping', the lazy way to prevent synthetic ropes unravelling is to simply melt the end, either with a hot knife or flame. Quick and temporarily effective though this might be, if you want it to stay secure in the long term it should be backed up with a properly made whipping.

Common whipping

This is not the most durable of whippings, but it can be done in minutes without special implements and is suitable for both 3-strand and braided ropes.

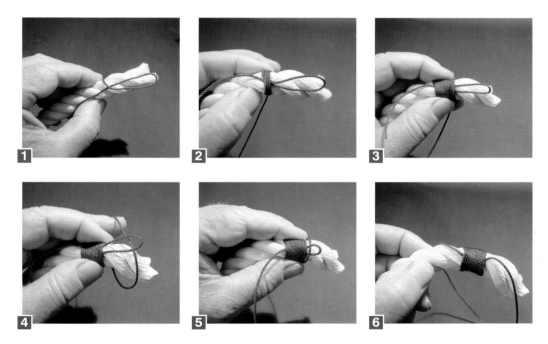

1   **You need a length of waxed whipping twine – say about 1m long for a 12mm diameter rope, other sizes as appropriate. Starting at a little less than two diameters from the end, lay a small bight of twine along the rope.**

2 & 3   **Now start whipping firmly towards the end – against the lay of the rope for 3-strand. Each turn should lie neatly against the previous one, covering the bight as you proceed.**

4 & 5   **Once you have whipped a length approximately equal to the diameter, pass the last turn of the twine through the loop made by the exposed bight ….**

6   **…. and then pull the bight back down under the whipping, thereby burying the working end. Snip off the surplus and you're done.**

Palm and needle whipping

This one will never let you down but you will need a sailmaker's needle and – ideally – a palm (available from chandlers) to push it through. With a little ingenuity you can manage without the palm. This whipping was originally intended for 3-strand rope but the principles can be adapted to braided ones as well. It employs what's known as 'frapping'– diagonal turns that cinch the whole whipping together.

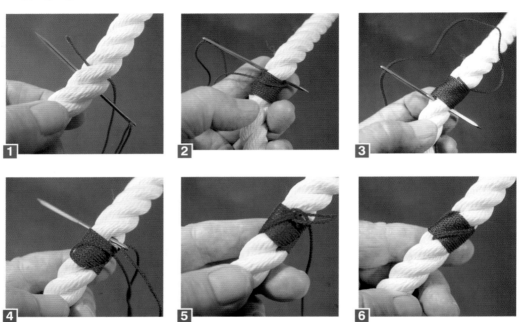

1   Thread your needle with waxed twine. With 3-strand, it's important that the rope doesn't unlay so start a good three diameters from the end.

2   Take a double pass through one of the strands to anchor the end of the twine then, as with the common whipping, whip against the lay for a length equal to the diameter.

3   Once satisfied with the length, identify the same strand you started with at the bottom, and push the needle under it, this time working with the lay – that's to say, back in the opposite direction.

4   The next stage is really the heart of the whole splice. Your needle will have emerged at end of a 'score' – the valleys between the strands. Follow the score down to the other end of the whipping, pass the needle under the next strand and return to the top. Repeat this process with each strand in turn until all three scores have a double frapping.

5 & 6 The last frapping turn should bring you down to the bottom of the whipping. Take a half hitch around the adjacent strand and pull it tight. As a final belt-and-braces precaution, take a couple of extra stitches back and forth through the rope before snipping the twine off close.

EYE SPLICE

There are many types of splices for 3-strand rope but the most useful by far is the eye splice. Although it looks complicated, it's actually very simple. A 'Swedish fid' is a useful tool to open up the strands but on smallish ropes you can often manage without.

Unlay sufficient rope to make the tucks and tape the ends (masking tape works well) to stop them unravelling. We will call these the working strands to distinguish them from those in the body of the rope.

1 & 2 Form the eye and arrange two working strands on top of the rope and one below. Note that the top ones fall naturally across (rather than along) the lay of the rope. Using a fid to open up the lay, tuck the top working strands under as shown here. Make sure that they pass under different but neighbouring strands.

3 Now turn the splice over. This time the remaining working strand matches the lay of the rope. This can be confusing. To make the third tuck it will help to consult the photo. See that the tuck is made in such a way as to reverse the working strand's natural lie, turning it through 90°.

4 & 5 You have completed the first series of tucks and the working strands should be evenly spaced around the rope, each emerging from a different score. From here on it's simply a matter of making three more sets of tucks, continuing against the lay on an 'over one, under one' basis. All that then remains is to trim off the surplus.

ROPEWORK

CLEATS

Cleats are another device with a history stretching back through the centuries. Yet, despite being a miracle of functional simplicity, they are often misused, as a stroll along any quayside will reveal.

They can serve in many roles, but on angling boats are most commonly there for securing mooring lines. Actually, the task of making fast the lines is easily done since winding almost any mess of rope around a cleat will probably hold. But making fast is only half the story. It's equally important that you can release a line at any time – even when under load. To return to your boat to find that the tide has gone out and your mooring lines are now as taut as bow strings could have you reaching for your filleting knife!

The problem probably started with the first turn, which should be a simple wrap around the cleat under the horns. It's vital that the rope should have a 'fair' lead onto the cleat as in Fig 5:1. If the lead is as in Fig 5:2 it's easy to imagine how the rope could jam when you lay on more turns.

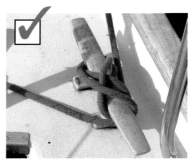

Fig 5:1 Fair lead to cleat

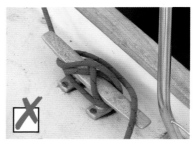

Fig 5:2 Foul lead to cleat

ALLOWING FOR TIDES

We shall be looking at tides in more detail later but no reference to cleats and loaded ropes should pass without some mention of the problems of lying alongside a wall in tidal waters.

Of course, we would all prefer to find some sort of floating pontoon arrangement, thoughtfully provided to do away with the tidal influences completely, but this isn't always possible. With thoughts of perhaps visiting a local pub in mind, most of us eventually find ourselves tying up to some inviting quayside or other.

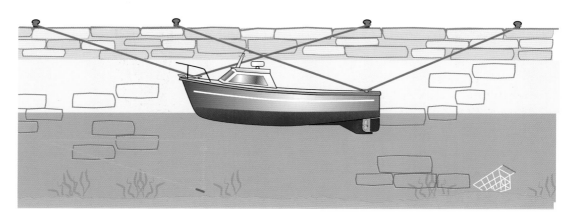

The trick is to use long mooring lines – within reason the longer the better. When the tide starts to fall, very short lines will come under tension almost immediately, whereas longer lines will be less affected. There are two reasons for this. When run to bollards some distance away, the angle of the mooring lines change less as the boat drops. Secondly, the extra length means there will be more stretch available – particularly so with nylon lines.

It also helps if you can secure the lines as close above the high water mark as possible. Some quays have rings for just this purpose.

ROPE HANDLING

In his hilarious account of a trip up the Thames in the 1880s, Jerome K Jerome – author of Three Men in a Boat – wrote 'I firmly believe that if you took an average tow-line and stretched it straight across the middle of a field, and then turned your back on it for thirty seconds, when you looked round again you would find it had got itself altogether in a heap...'.

How true – not just of tow-lines but of ropes in general. Indispensable though they certainly are, they're inclined to be unruly. The only way to keep them tamed is to stow them away properly in the first place.

Coiling

A tradition born of practical experience is that ropes should be coiled in a clockwise direction – that's to say clockwise when coiling with your right hand into your left. This arises from the construction of 3-strand ropes which have a tendency to kink if coiled the other way. Actually there's no reason why braided ropes shouldn't be coiled anti-clockwise, but it's better to get into the habit of following the convention so it becomes second nature to you. Since it requires only modest dexterity, left-handed folk are advised to do the job right-handed.

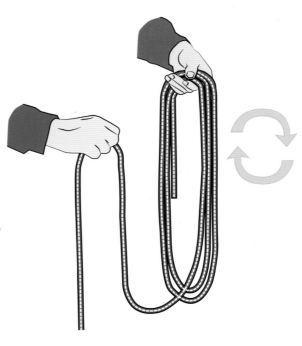

With each turn you make, it's important to give the rope a slight twist between thumb and forefinger to allow it to lie comfortably against the proceeding turns. If the rope is in use – perhaps a mooring line – start at the point where it's made fast. If you start at the free end, kinks will develop as you near the cleat.

Of course, large ropes are too heavy to be coiled into your hand. These should be coiled onto the deck – again clockwise with a little twist to ease the way.

Gasket coil hitch

Having neatly coiled your rope, naturally you would like it to stay that way. Large ropes should be secured with 'stops' – bootlace lengths of twine tied at intervals around the coil.

For lighter ropes there's the gasket coil hitch.

1   **Close the coil so it can be held in one hand and, with the other hand, take a few neat turns around it.**

2   **As you approach the free end, form a small loop and pass it through the 'eye' of the coil.**

3   **Recover the loop from the other side, then simply bring it forward and drop it over the head of the coil. Cinch it tight and you're done.**

1

2

3

Heaving lines

A heaving line is a light rope – 6mm diameter is ideal – usually used as a messenger to pass a heavier rope across a gap, either between your boat and the shore or perhaps to another boat. An example of the latter could be when rigging a tow-line. The end of the line should have a soft weight – traditionally made up of a knot called a 'monkey's fist'.

■   Coil the line clockwise as usual, then divide the coil in two so you have a half in each hand. Right-handers should have the monkey's fist end in their right hand and vice-versa. Either tie off the other end or stand on it so it won't be lost. The second coil should be held in the open palm of your non-throwing hand so it can run free.

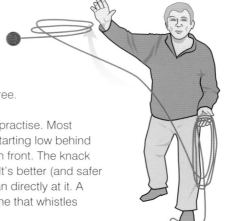

■   The actual heaving requires some skill so it helps to practise. Most people use a sort of underarm throw with their arm starting low behind them and ending a little above shoulder height and in front. The knack lies in releasing the coil at exactly the right moment. It's better (and safer for all concerned) to throw over your target rather than directly at it. A line that falls short is impossible to catch, whereas one that whistles overhead can be retrieved without difficulty.

Chapter 6

TOWING

Engines can be unreliable beasts so the likelihood is that sooner or later you will be involved in towing – whether as the 'tug' or the 'tow'. Although the tug has the more responsible role, this doesn't mean the tow can simply relax and enjoy the ride. Both have to work together to make the operation successful.

In any form of towing, the loads on the towrope can be high, particularly if conditions are rough. In such circumstances the surging caused by wave action can produce horrendous snatch loads. The ideal towrope should be both strong and stretchy – nylon being the best choice. It also helps if the towrope is as long as is practicable – better still if the length can be adjusted so the tug and tow are two wave crests apart, allowing both boats to rise and plunge at the same moment. Many skippers find that their anchor warp serves well.

Unless the sea is very calm, the tug should avoid coming alongside to either pass or receive the towrope. The safer option is to use a heaving line as described on page 42.

Finally, it's important to do what you can to minimise chafe. This might involve padding fairleads or other areas of contact with rags or similar. But watch out for your fingers as you do so! The slackening and tightening of a towrope can cause serious injury to the unwary.

Being the tug

Commercial tugs, marina workboats and other vessels that tow regularly are almost always fitted with a central bollard (Fig 6:1). Terminating the load at the tug's mid-point allows the stern to swing from side to side, which means that the tug can more easily be steered. The towrope is traditionally secured with a tugboat hitch around the bollard but, unfortunately, this is rarely possible on recreational craft, who must make do with what they have.

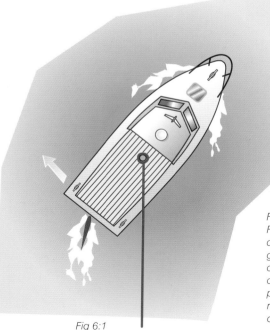

Fig 6:1

Fig 6:2 Tugboat hitch
For simplicity's sake this drawing only gives the general idea. In reality three or four more loops are dropped over the post, first going round behind from one direction then the other

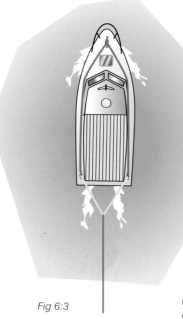

Fig 6:3

We've talked about the need for a strong towrope but even the strongest will be useless if the cleats are too flimsy. The stoutest cleat or bollard is typically the one used to secure the anchor rode but, of course, it's up in the bow and therefore of little help when towing. A useful compromise is to rig a bridle from the stern cleats, backed up with a pair of lines from forward (Fig 6:3).

Keep your speed down

If the tug is larger and potentially faster then the tow, a serious problem can arise. Back in Chapter 1 (page 11) we saw that the maximum speed of a displacement type boat is called 'hull speed' and that this is limited by waterline length. To put this point in context, a boat with a 20ft (6.1m) waterline will be capable of only about 6 knots while one having a 40ft waterline will do nearly 8.5 knots.

Now imagine the larger boat towing the smaller one flat out (Fig 6:4). The tow will be travelling 2.5 knots faster than its hull speed and its stern will have sunk into the trough behind its bow wave. In extreme cases the water could slosh over its transom and the boat would be swamped. Planing type boats may be less susceptible but even they can experience more than the usual degree of excitement.

It's therefore essential that the tug matches its speed to one that's comfortable for the tow. In practice, this will be well below the smaller boat's hull speed – say, no more than 5 knots for our example. Not only will this greatly reduce the resistance – and thereby the load on the towrope – but it will ensure a kindly-meant rescue doesn't turn into a tragedy of its own making.

In brief:

■ Take up the strain gradually then keep your speed down. If you see water boiling up behind the tow's transom, you are going too fast. Remember that a large, powerful boat can pull a smaller one under vert quickly.

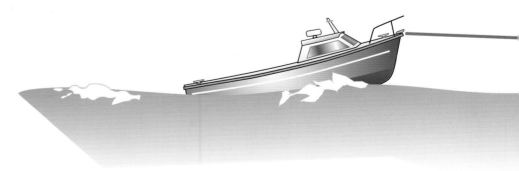

Fig 6:4

- Keep a close eye on the tow at all times and inspect the towrope regularly for chafe. Watch for signals that the tow is experiencing difficulties.

- Avoid abrupt changes in course that could put a side load on the tow. Alter course smoothly in a gentle arc.

Being towed

Although hopefully blessed with a hefty cleat or bollard forward, you still can't be sure that it (or the deck it's attached to) will be strong enough. So, once again, it's worth backing up the towrope by rigging lines taken back to secondary strong points – either cleats or maybe parts of the boat's structure (Fig 6:5). Alternatively, you could use a bridle to spread the load. It all depends on the boat and where the cleats are sited.

And don't forget that constant enemy, chafe – which will be more of a problem for you than for the tug, particularly at your bow where the towrope comes aboard. Ideally, your boat will have a smoothly profiled bow fairlead (a deck fitting used to guide a rope) but many haven't. Protect the rope with short lengths of flexible hose or pad it with rags. In brief:

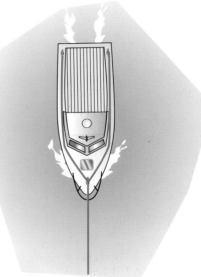

- Try and secure the towrope and any back-up lines so they can be released quickly. Watch out for foul leads to cleats (see page 40) which can jam under load. If in doubt, keep a serrated knife handy.

Fig 6:5

- Steer as if following in the wake of the tug. The lumpier the seas, the harder you will have to concentrate.

Agree salvage

The fellowship of the sea usually means that help will be offered freely – but that isn't always so, particularly if your rescuer is a commercial vessel whose work is disrupted. So broach the subject in advance and agree terms. Often a contribution towards fuel or a couple of beers will suffice.

Alongside towing

Because the tug can manoeuvre both boats almost as nimbly as one – including stopping and going astern – this is a useful technique in confined circumstances such as harbours and marinas.

    The key to success lies firstly in the relative position of the two craft, and then how you secure them together. Start by rigging lots of fenders to cushion the inevitable surging that will occur.

Then proceed as follows:

■ Where possible, the tug's stern should protrude aft of the towed boat's. This simple trick helps a lot with manoeuvrability because the tug can exert more leverage.

■ How you rig the securing lines will depend on the positions of the cleats and other strong points on each boat. The most important lines are the springs which will bear almost all the load when going forward and astern. The bow and stern lines are there mainly to hold the 'raft' together. Something like the arrangement shown in Fig 6:6 will work well.

■ As with a conventional tow, it's better if both boats are steered together. Since the tug skipper is ultimately in control, it's he who should coordinate the manoeuvres. Communication is everything. This is no time to ignore the other and go your own way.

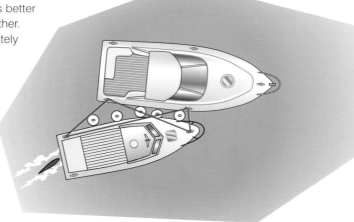

■ Even if both boats are helmed, the asymmetric thrust and drag will still make it difficult to maintain a straight course. The tug skipper will find himself having to steer his stern in

Fig 6:6

towards the towed boat to compensate. However, this awkwardness can be used to advantage when manoeuvring. Whether going astern or ahead, it's much easier to make a turn in the direction of the tow than away from it. To take further advantage of this effect, a tug with a right-handed prop should be on the starboard side of the tow so the prop-walk will assist when going astern.

Chapter 7

COLLISION AVOIDANCE

To the casual observer, the sea is an unregulated expanse on which you can do just about anything you like. To some extent this is true but it only takes a moment's thought to realise that there must be some rules governing our actions. And there are. The most important of them are covered by the International Regulations for Preventing Collision at Sea (often known as the IRPCS or, less formally, the 'Colregs'). These define our responsibilities to ourselves and other seafarers and specify how we should act whenever there's a risk of collision.

It must be emphasised that the regulations apply to all vessels, from the largest ships to the tiniest dinghies. It's the legal responsibility of every skipper to comply.

Is there a collision risk?

Clearly, if two vessels are approaching each other head to head, action is necessary – and soon, because their combined speeds are bringing them together. Less obvious is where you spot a boat on a converging course. Fortunately, there's a useful trick to see if a risk exists. If the boat appears to be getting closer but its relative bearing remains the same, then sooner or later you will meet.

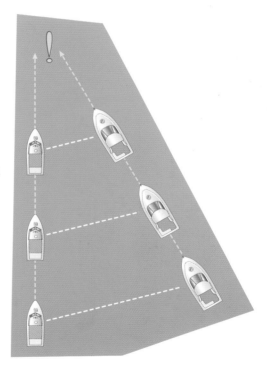

Before we look at specific examples, a few words of explanation. For most circumstances the rules talk of the 'give way vessel' and the 'stand on vessel', the latter being that which has the 'right of way'. However, there are no absolute rights. It is the duty of both skippers to avoid collision at all costs. So, should things deteriorate to the point where collision looks probable, the stand on boat must take whatever action it can to avert an accident.

And, common sense has its place. That enormous container ship charging down on you might technically be the give way vessel, but it would be a very foolish angling boat skipper who put that to the test by standing on his rights.

REMEMBER: There's no such thing as an emergency stop for large vessels. Neither can they turn quickly. Always act in good time.

THE RULES OF THE ROAD

The IRPCS starts with some general requirements:

■ The rules apply to all vessels on the high seas. Note that such bodies as harbour and river authorities may have their own regulations.

■ You must maintain a proper lookout at all times.

■ Every vessel shall proceed at a safe speed. In other words, skippers must consider such potential hazards as poor visibility, navigational obstructions and traffic density.

■ Actions to avoid collision should be made early and in an obvious manner – by which is meant that it should be clear to other vessels what your intentions are. Altering course 5° might not be noticed, whereas 20° or so certainly would.

Now let's look at how the rules apply in common situations.

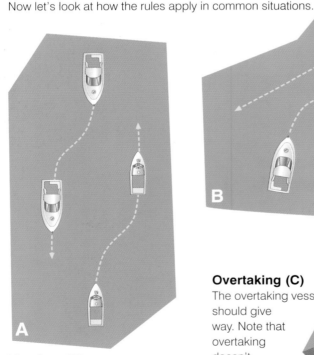

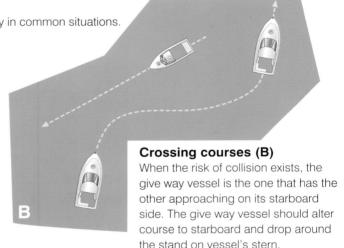

Crossing courses (B)
When the risk of collision exists, the give way vessel is the one that has the other approaching on its starboard side. The give way vessel should alter course to starboard and drop around the stand on vessel's stern.

Overtaking (C)
The overtaking vessel should give way. Note that overtaking doesn't just mean approaching from dead astern. Any vessel gaining on another from anywhere within a 135° arc must give way. This arc coincides with that shown by a sternlight (see page 51).

Head on (A)
There is no stand on vessel in this situation. Each boat must make a clearly obvious turn to starboard so that they pass each other port side to port side.

When power and sail meet

It's commonly believed that 'steam (power) gives way to sail' but this isn't always true. If a sailing yacht is overtaking you, it becomes the give way vessel. And, if it's sailing with assistance from the engine – a popular technique known as motor-sailing – then it becomes a motor vessel and must behave accordingly. When motor-sailing in daylight, yachts should hoist a downward-pointing black cone, but too often don't bother – a blatant and unfair breach of the regulations.

It might seem to powerboaters that sailing yachts sometimes behave in irrational and unpredictable ways, so it helps to understand their limitations. The big problem is that they can't sail directly upwind and must therefore 'tack' – a manoeuvre involving sailing at about 45° to the wind in a series of zigzags (Fig 7:1). Another hindrance is their draught. The keel of a typical 12m sailing yacht extends about 2m below water level which means it can't venture into the shallows. A yacht's erratic course – more likely inshore – may be due to it following deeper channels or avoiding underwater obstructions that you can ignore (Fig 7:2).

Much of seamanship is about showing consideration for others. A fair-minded yachtsman would give an angling boat a wide berth so his keel doesn't foul their lines. To be courteous in return reinforces cooperation amongst seamen.

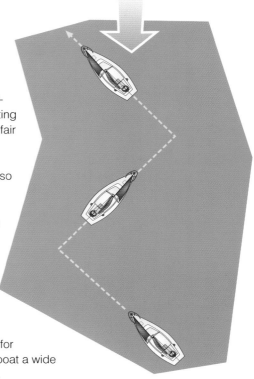

Fig 7:1

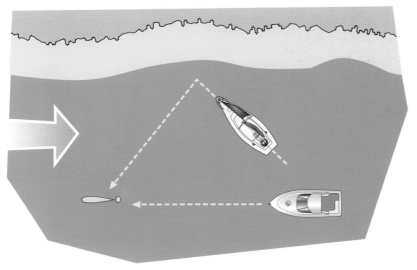

Fig 7:2

Rules for narrow channels

Considering how congested they can become, it's hardly surprising that the rules become stricter for narrow channels. Equally surprising is how often the rules are ignored.

The IRPCS (International Regulations for Preventing Collision at Sea) rule that spells out what our responsibilities are is Rule 9. It's worth looking at its contents in detail.

- *'A vessel proceeding along the course of a narrow channel or fairway shall keep as near to the outer limit of the channel or fairway which lies on her starboard side as is safe or practicable.'*
  Basically, these means that all vessels should drive on the right and keep the centre of the channel as free as possible.

- *'A vessel of less than 20 metres in length or a sailing vessel shall not impede the passage of a vessel which can safely navigate only within a narrow channel or fairway.'*
  This is no more than common sense. Larger vessels need the deeper water and it's only right that we let them have it.

- *'A vessel engaged in fishing shall not impede the passage of any other vessel navigating within a narrow channel or fairway.'*
  A sentence of particular interest to anglers. Note that it doesn't say you shouldn't fish – only that 'you shall not impede' and, what's more, that you shall not impede 'any other vessel'. Narrow channels often mean good fishing – but you have a duty not to obstruct other boats or ships passing through them.

- *'A vessel shall not cross a narrow channel or fairway if such crossing impedes the passage of a vessel which can navigate safely only within such channel or fairway.'*
  More common sense. Large vessels have very poor brakes, so don't risk crossing close in front of them. Let them pass before crossing.

Finally, before we leave this subject, in any situation where you see a ship approaching and hear five short blasts from her whistle (horn) it means that it thinks it might hit you. Get out of the way!

LIGHTS, SHAPES AND FOG SIGNALS

During the day it's usually quite easy to judge the size, type, speed and course of another vessel, but that's not the case at night. To make this possible all vessels carry distinguishing lights after dark. Even in daylight a vessel might be engaged in some activity that isn't very obvious. In those circumstances, a vessel must display a shape or shapes – always black – to signal what's going on.

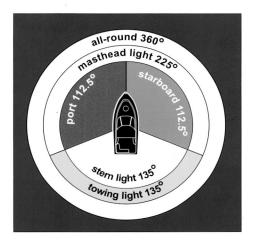

Fig 7:3

Sound signals are most commonly made with a 'whistle' – better known as a 'fog-horn' when talking of large ships. They aren't as informative as lights or shapes but they do give some indication of what might be out there with you and in what direction danger might lie. A 'short blast' means one approximately 1 second long. A 'prolonged blast' should be somewhere between 4–6 seconds.

Lights are characterised by their colour and the arc through which they can be seen (Fig 7:3). Obviously, 'all-round' lights can be seen through 360°.

The basic lights are intended to indicate in which general direction another vessel is heading. They are:

- **Masthead light** A white light that can be seen from dead ahead to 22.5° abaft the beam on either side – a total arc of 225°. Vessels over 50m must carry two as shown below.

- **Sidelights** Often called 'port and starboard lights'. The port light is red and can be seen from dead ahead to 22.5° abaft the beam to port. The starboard light is green and displays over the same arc to starboard.

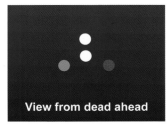

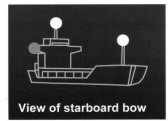

- **Sternlight** A white light – usually mounted aft – displaying through an arc of 67.5° from dead astern on both sides – a total of 135°.

Note that the sternlight fills in the 'gap' left by the masthead light. This means that if you can see the stern light, you shouldn't be able to see the masthead light or sidelights. Conversely, if you see a sidelight and masthead lights, the sternlight should be invisible to you.

Able to manoeuvre freely

- A vessel of less than 7m doing less than 7 knots displays a single all-round white light. Note that this could be mistaken for a vessel at anchor or one seen from astern.

- A powered craft under 50m displays sidelights, a white masthead light and a white stern light. Under 12m the last two can be combined in a single all-round tricolour light.
  Fog: ⬤ every two minutes.

- A powered craft over 50m – probably a ship! – carries sidelights, a sternlight and two masthead lights – the forward one being lower than the after one.
  Fog: ⬤ every two minutes.

- A yacht under sail shows sidelights and a sternlight. These can either be separate lights or combined in a tricolour light at the masthead. When under power (whether the sails are up or not) it becomes a power vessel and must show the appropriate lights.
  A yacht motor-sailing in daylight must carry a black cone shape pointing downwards (Fig 7:4).
  Fog: ⬤ ● ● every two minutes (when under sail).

Fig 7:4

This yacht is motor sailing. Note the absence of a cone – a common breach of the regulations

Restricted or unable to manoeuvre

- A vessel under 50m at anchor displays a single all-round white light.
  By day it shows a black ball.
  Fog: ▬ ● ● every two minutes.

- A vessel over 50m at anchor displays an all-round white light at both the bow and stern. The light at the stern is mounted lower. By day it shows a single black ball.

  Fog: <100m rapid ringing of bell for 5 seconds every minute.

  >100m also a gong aft for 5 seconds in every minute.

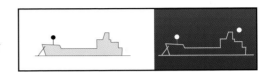

- Diving boats show Code Flag A during the day and by night display the lights of 'a vessel restricted in her ability to manoeuvre'.
  Fog: ▬ ● ● every two minutes.

- A vessel not under command – perhaps engine or steering failure – displays two all-round red lights, one above the other. By day two black balls are shown.
  Fog: ▬ ● ● every two minutes.

- If constrained by draught, three all-round red lights in a vertical line are displayed, as well as the usual lights if under way. The day shape is a black cylinder.
  Fog: ▬ ● ● every two minutes.

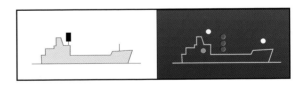

- When restricted in her ability to manoeuvre (grimly abbreviated to RAM) a vessel also shows three all-round lights but the middle one is white. The day shapes are ball, diamond, ball – again vertically.
  Fog: ▬ ● ● every two minutes.

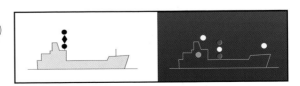

Vessels at work

- Fishing vessels (except trawlers) carry the usual sidelights and sternlight for power vessels under way with two additional lights – an all-round red mounted above an all-round white. By day they show a couple of cones mounted apex to apex.
  Fog: ▬ ● ● every two minutes.

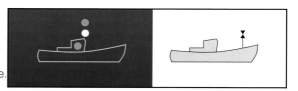

- When trawling, a vessel carries an all-round green light over a white light, along with the usual sidelights and sternlight for a power vessel under way. The day shapes are two cones as above.
  Fog: ▬ ● ● every two minutes.

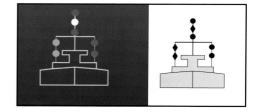

- Dredgers show the same vertical red, white, red lights as vessels restricted in their ability to manoeuvre, plus two vertical reds and two vertical greens at either side. The green lights indicate which side is safe to pass. The day shapes are, again, the same as our RAM, plus two balls and two diamonds at either side. The diamonds indicate the safe side.
  Fog: ▬ ● ● every two minutes.

- It's important to recognise a towing operation because you can't always see the towrope which may be partially immersed. The lights and shapes depend on the overall length of the tow – measured from the stern of the tug to the after end of the tow.

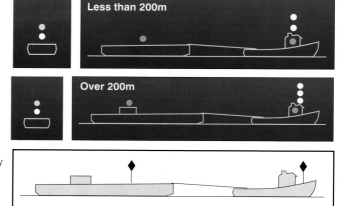

Less than 200m: Along with the usual power vessel lights, the tug carries a second white masthead light and a yellow towing light above the sternlight and displaying over the same arc. The tow shows sidelights and sternlight.

Over 200m: As above but with a third masthead light. By day tug and tow each show a black diamond shape.
Fog: ▬ ● ● every two minutes.

■ When on duty, pilot vessels carry sidelights and sternlight plus all-round white and red lights mounted vertically. By day they fly a white and red flag. In both cases white is uppermost. These are primarily for recognition purposes, since pilot vessels can usually manoeuvre freely.

Fog: ● ● ● ●

Light fantastic

Other lights may be seen. Some very fast craft choose to display flashing lights. However, this is not legal, except for hovercraft and then the light must be yellow. Working lights can be a distraction. Cruise liners and ferries can have rows of brightly lit windows and dredgers and commercial fishing vessels can be ablaze with floodlights.

Unfortunately, the reality at sea is that it's quite common to see non-standard lights or to have difficulty picking out the important ones from all the others. In such circumstances, the prudent skipper should play safe and stay clear.

Sound sense

A very dangerous state of affairs arises when one vessel doesn't know the intentions of another. Sound signals can be used to clarify the situation.

● **One short blast:** 'I am turning to starboard.'

● ● **Two short blasts:** 'I am turning to port.'

● ● ● **Three short blasts:** 'My engines are going astern.' Note that it refers only to the 'engines'. Large vessels are slow to react and might still be moving forward.

● ● ● ● ● **Five short blasts:** 'I don't understand your intentions.' This can be interpreted as 'what the heck are you doing?' Or stronger.

Traffic separation schemes appear on charts as purple lines and shaded areas. The arrows show the direction of each shipping lane. Crossing vessels must do so at 90° to the traffic flow – making no course adjustment for tidal stream and never at an oblique angle.

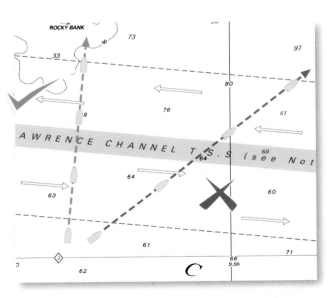

Chapter 8

BUOYS, LIGHTS AND MARKS

Whereas the IRPCS is consistent worldwide, buoyage systems are split into two groups, both overseen by the International Association of Lighthouse Authorities (IALA). Across Europe, Russia, India, Africa, Australia, New Zealand and much of the Western Pacific, IALA 'A' is used. IALA 'B' is the system in North and South America, Japan, Korea, the Philippines and some of the Caribbean.

Parts of the two systems are identical, but there are also some very significant differences.

Cardinal marks

These are the same for both IALA 'A' and IALA 'B'. Cardinal marks warn of danger and indicate the position of the mark relative to that danger. The cone top marks always point towards the black bands (Fig 8:1).

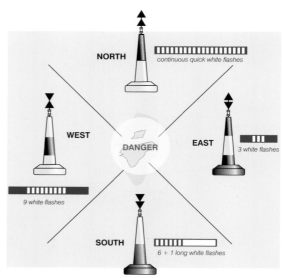

Fig 8:1

IALA - 'A' Buoyage system

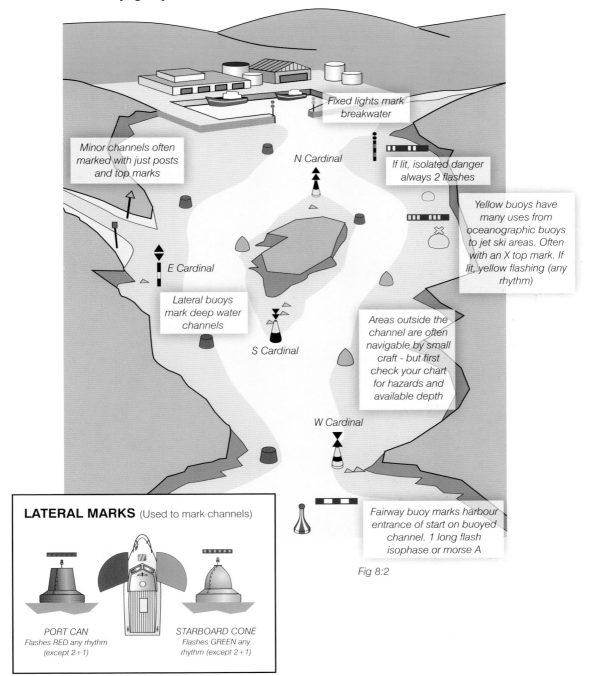

Fixed lights mark breakwater

Minor channels often marked with just posts and top marks

N Cardinal

If lit, isolated danger always 2 flashes

Yellow buoys have many uses from oceanographic buoys to jet ski areas. Often with an X top mark. If lit, yellow flashing (any rhythm)

E Cardinal

Lateral buoys mark deep water channels

S Cardinal

Areas outside the channel are often navigable by small craft - but first check your chart for hazards and available depth

W Cardinal

Fairway buoy marks harbour entrance of start on buoyed channel. 1 long flash isophase or morse A

Fig 8:2

LATERAL MARKS (Used to mark channels)

PORT CAN
Flashes RED any rhythm (except 2 + 1)

STARBOARD CONE
Flashes GREEN any rhythm (except 2 + 1)

IALA - 'B' Buoyage system

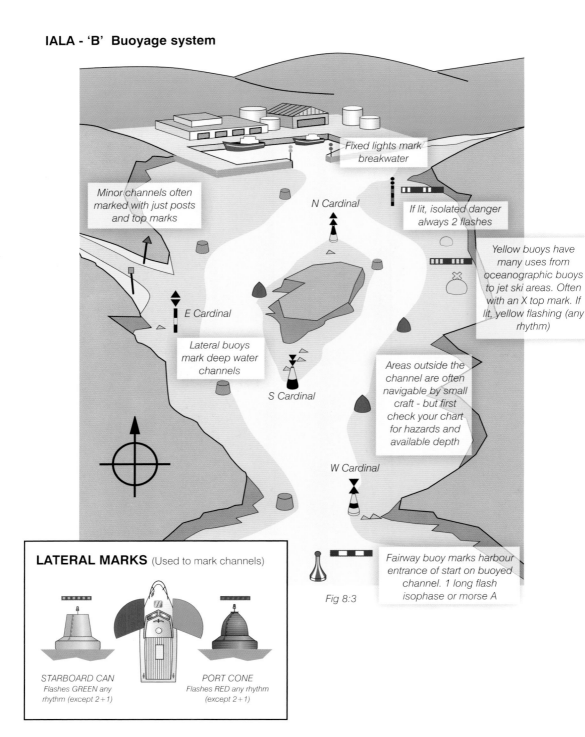

Fixed lights mark breakwater

Minor channels often marked with just posts and top marks

N Cardinal

If lit, isolated danger always 2 flashes

Yellow buoys have many uses from oceanographic buoys to jet ski areas. Often with an X top mark. If lit, yellow flashing (any rhythm)

E Cardinal

Lateral buoys mark deep water channels

S Cardinal

Areas outside the channel are often navigable by small craft - but first check your chart for hazards and available depth

W Cardinal

LATERAL MARKS (Used to mark channels)

STARBOARD CAN
Flashes GREEN any rhythm (except 2+1)

PORT CONE
Flashes RED any rhythm (except 2+1)

Fairway buoy marks harbour entrance of start on buoyed channel. 1 long flash isophase or morse A

Fig 8:3

Light characteristics

	Name	Chart Symbol	Description
	Fixed	F	Fixed light – always on.
	Flashing	Fl	Flashing, more off than on.
	Group flashing	Fl(2)	Flashing – in this case in groups of 2.
	Long flashing	LFl	Flashing, more off than on, but flashes longer than 2 seconds.
	Quick	Q	50-79 flashes per min.
	Very quick	VQ	80-90 flashes per min.
	Group quick	Q(4)	A group of quick flashes followed by a period off.
	Interrupted quick	IQ	Similar to group quick but with no specified number of flashes.
	Isophase	Iso	Equal on and off.
	Occulting	Oc	More on than off.
	Alternating	Al.WR	Colour changes – in this case white and red.
	Fixed and flashing	F Fl(4)	Fixed light with flashes of higher intensity.

Sectored Lights

The white sector of a sectored light indicates the safe path. Entering from seaward, if you see a red light you are too far to port; a green light means you are too far to starboard.

Sometimes one sectored light will lead you safely to another. Again, simply follow the white path.

Chapter 9

NAVIGATION

Ashore on our home turf, we rely on familiar landmarks to find our way around – left at the church will take us to the pub, and so on. This is done without thinking; our local knowledge is ingrained. Then, when we stray further afield, we switch our trust to road signs and maps and there's often a stranger who can give us directions.

Not so at sea, where there's a bewildering lack of road signs and no handy bloke to point the way. But at least there are maps – or 'charts' as they are called. And these have been trusted guides to sailors for centuries.

Traditional charts are printed on paper, but the trend today is more and more towards electronics – the modern chart plotter, with all its wonderful functions – and, of course, its potential unreliability.

Latitude and longitude

Any location can be pinpointed by its latitude and longitude. Both are angular measurements (in degrees, minutes, and seconds) taken from the Earth's centre: vertically north and south from the equator; and horizontally in a westward direction from the prime (Greenwich) meridian. When these angles are extended to the Earth's surface, they produce lines of latitude and longitude – a huge imaginary grid stretching from pole to pole.

This grid is reproduced on every chart but, of course, there's an obvious snag. Charts are flat while the Earth is round. And, whereas the lines of latitude are equally spaced, the lines of longitude converge until they meet at the poles – rather like the segments of an orange.

To overcome this problem, most charts use what's known as a Mercator projection (left), where all the lines are shown parallel. Since lines of longitude can't possibly be parallel, this can only be achieved by stretching horizontal distances – that's to say, in the east-west direction. This necessary distortion has an important bearing on how we use charts.

The red dot on the chart indicates the position 45°N 30°W shown on the globe, right

Nautical mile

Distances at sea are measured in nautical miles. Each mile is considered to be 1852 metres long – about 15% longer than the English statute mile. But a nautical mile started life as an angular measurement in exactly the same way as latitude was calculated – in fact, one nautical mile is equal to one minute of latitude and a 'knot' is a speed of 1 nautical mile per hour.

The practical significance of this is that degrees and minutes of latitude are shown on the side margins of all charts, and therefore distances can be measured by comparing them with the latitude scale – **but never the horizontal longitude scale which we know to be distorted.**

Incidentally, you will sometimes hear people refer to 'knots per hour' – clearly nonsensical since it would mean nautical miles per hour per hour!

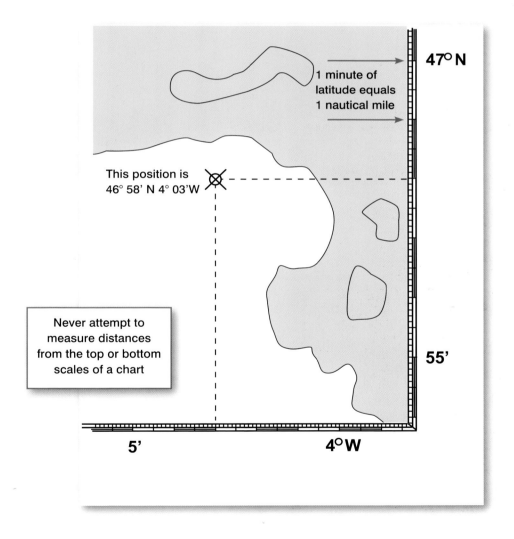

1 minute of latitude equals 1 nautical mile

47° N

This position is 46° 58' N 4° 03'W

Never attempt to measure distances from the top or bottom scales of a chart

55'

5'

4° W

The compass

The first written reference to a magnetic compass goes back nearly a thousand years and there's good reason to believe they were in use well before then.

The basic compass is a very simple device. A magnetised needle is allowed to pivot freely and will align itself with the Earth's magnetic field – more or less north and south. Unfortunately, 'more or less', isn't really good enough for navigation. The compass is pointing to the magnetic north pole, currently located (it moves slowly with time) about 600 miles from the true north pole. This produces an error known as 'variation'. Variation isn't constant but differs from place to place. The amount for each locality (and its rate of change, usually small enough to ignore) is noted on your chart's 360° 'compass rose'.

Another form of error is called 'deviation'. This is caused by magnetic disturbances caused by the boat itself: cast iron engine blocks, electrical equipment and so on. Steel boats have a particular problem. It's possible to measure the deviation by 'swinging the compass' but most of us simply minimise its effects by mounting the compass as far away as is practicable from any object that might disturb it. Incidentally, electronic fluxgate type compasses can identify deviation for themselves – a very useful procedure.

Whatever the source of the error, corrections must be made before we can truly know what course we are steering. An easily remembered rule can help us here – based on a single word:

CADET

This reminds us that when converting from compass (C) to true (T) we have to add (AD) east (E) – and of course west must be subtracted.

BASIC CHARTWORK

A common belief is that charts are only for offshore vessels. Nothing could be further from the truth. A ship crossing an ocean could navigate between two points without referring to a chart at all – there's nothing out there, after all. It's inshore that we need the most information.

The purpose of charts is twofold. Firstly, they warn us of any dangers and, secondly, they allow us to practise the art of navigation – which we can think of as travelling safely from one place to another. As a bonus to anglers, charts also show us where wrecks, shallows and other good fishing spots are to be found.

Position finding

Much of navigation relies on knowing where we are. Although these days there's a growing reliance on GPS (Global Positioning System) it's still important that we don't depend on it entirely. The traditional method

Fig 9:1

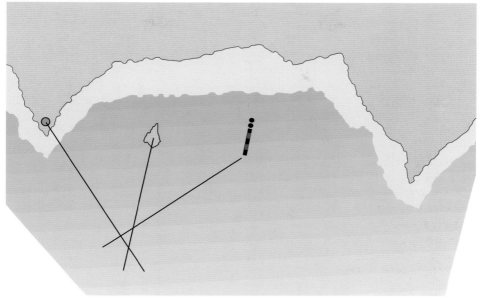

Fig 9:2

was to use a 'hand bearing' compass – a small, portable compass with some form of sighting arrangement (Fig 9:1). By taking bearings of prominent objects and plotting them on our chart, we can establish our position. A minimum of two bearings will produce a 'fix', but three or more is better. Remember that your bearings will have to be corrected for variation (and deviation if known) and don't worry if the lines don't cross at exactly the same point – they rarely do, the resulting triangle being known as a 'cocked hat' (Fig 9:2).

Setting a course

Once you know where you are, the next step might be to set a course to another spot. You start by drawing a line (a 2b pencil is easy to erase) between your position and your destination (Fig

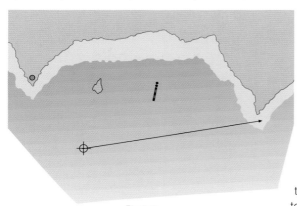

Fig 9:3

9:3). There are various methods of measuring the angle of your course, but the handiest on small boats is one of the navigational protractors – either the Douglas or Breton type being a good choice. Having determined your true course, allowance must be made for variation to obtain a compass course. Simply reverse the CADET rule described on page 64. That's to say easterly variation should be subtracted and westerly added. Incidentally, Breton type plotters can be used in such a way as to do this automatically.

TIDES

In the previous section our course went directly from point to point as if the sea was fixed and static. No allowances were made for tidal stream which, for many of us, would mean that if we blindly steered the compass course we would be swept aside and would miss our destination.

How tides occur

Not all of the world's seas are significantly tidal but, in those that are, they become a potent issue for navigators. Tides are caused by gravitational forces – more specifically, the gravitational pull of the moon and sun. Although the sun's mass makes for the mightier gravitational force, it's much further away so its effect is about equal to the moon's.

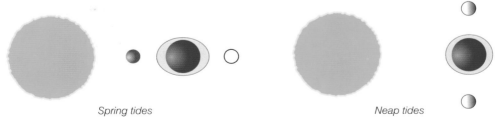

Spring tides   *Neap tides*

The word 'diurnal' means once a day. As the Earth spins on its axis, those waters directly under the moon are attracted upwards – creating a diurnal tide. But, hang on, you say – surely there are two tides per day? And you would be right. The reason for this is that there's a balancing effect on the other side of the globe – another, smaller bulge in the water matching the bulge under the moon. So, the reality is that we have two tides a day – semi-diurnal, in fact.

The sun's involvement affects the size of each tide in approximately two-week cycles. When both moon and sun line up, or when the sun and moon are on opposite sides of the Earth you get high 'spring' tides. And when they are at 90° to each other you get the lesser 'neaps'.

Tidal range

It's important to understand that spring and neap refer to variations in tidal range. At high and low water, a spring tide will be both higher and lower than a neap tide – i.e. it has the greater range. By comparison, neap tides won't dip as low nor rise as high – i.e. have a smaller range.

Tides are measured from a 'datum', an agreed level which in Britain and the rest of Europe is the Lowest Astronomical Tide (LAT). This is the lowest the tide can be expected to fall if we ignore temporary influences such as wind and barometric pressure. As well as LAT, other abbreviations are common. For example MHWS means Mean High Water Springs and stands for the average height of spring tides over a year. From piece of information, it shouldn't be hard to figure out the others on the drawing Fig 9:4.

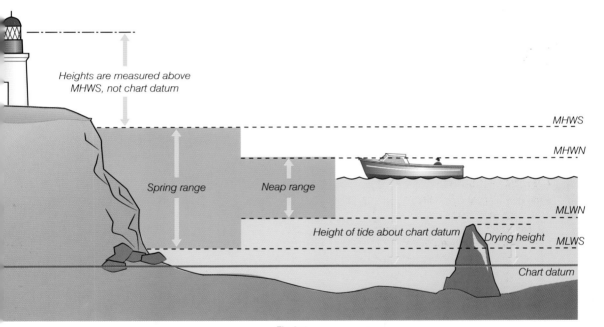

Fig 9:4

Allowing for tides

As we covered in Chapter 4, a tidal stream means we're operating on a platform of moving water. A simple example would be someone motoring at 6 knots with a stream of 1 knot from directly abeam. One hour later our boat will have moved 6nm (nautical miles) forward and been carried 1nm sideways by the stream. A boat doing 12 knots would motor twice the distance in the same time, but still would only be carried 1nm downstream. It follows that slower boats are more affected by tidal streams than faster ones.

There are ways of plotting stream effects and computing the course adjustments needed to overcome them but these are fiddly and unnecessary, except perhaps for very slow boats. However, there are some useful tricks which will serve instead.

Fair or foul tide

The first is obvious. If the stream is coming from dead ahead, it will slow the boat's speed by the rate of that stream. For example, our 12 knot boat facing a 2 knot tide would only make 10 knots over the ground. On the other hand, if the stream was from astern, the same boat would make 14 knots over the ground. Note that the difference between them is twice the speed of the tide.

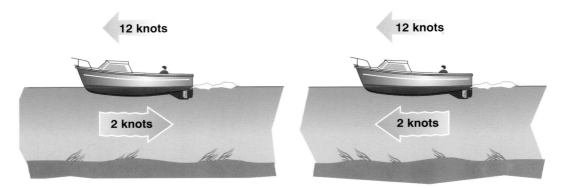

Cross tide

The second situation sees the tide abeam and is based on what's known as the 'one in sixty rule'. The rule says that a 1° course error would put you approximately 1nm off-track after a run of 60nm. A 10° course error would result in you being 10nm out of position and so on. It only works for relatively small angles of error but, by standing the rule on its head, we can estimate the course correction needed to hit our destination spot on. Some simple arithmetic is required.

$$\frac{\text{tide speed} \times 60}{\text{boat speed}} = \text{course correction}$$

For our 12 knot boat now living with a 2 knot cross tide, this would be:

$$\frac{2 \times 60}{12} = 10° \text{ course correction}$$

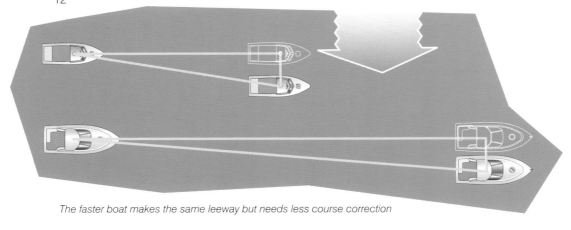

The faster boat makes the same leeway but needs less course correction

Bow tide

With the tide running against you at about 45° on the bow, we use the 'two-thirds rule'. This estimates that the tide will act two-thirds along the track and two-thirds across it as shown in Fig 9:5. At first this may seem confusing but let's assume a bow tide of 3 knots, two-thirds of which is 2 knots. You can then think of your boat as experiencing a 2 knot head tide and a 2 knot cross tide – both at the same time. This would mean that our 12 knot boat would only make 10 knots over the ground and would be carried 2nm downstream over an hour.

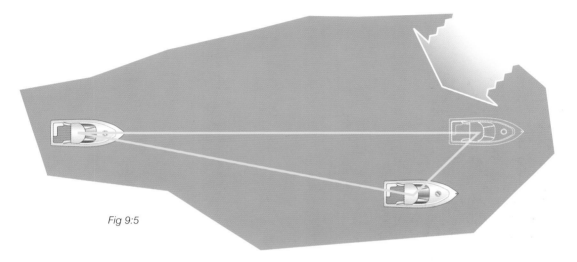

Fig 9:5

There's no point in being absolutely accurate. Tidal rates are only a prediction after all, and can be influenced by all sorts of unexpected events. Better by far to have a rough idea how the stream will affect you and then make a judgement as to what corrective action is about right in those circumstances.

Stream rates – 'rule of twelfths'

This rule doesn't belong in the same group as the previous ones, but is extremely useful for estimating the rate of rise and fall at any stage of the tide. It assumes that the time between LW and HW (or HW to LW) takes 6 hours, which isn't strictly accurate but is close enough for our purposes. Once the tide turns, it starts slowly, then gradually increases, finally slowing down again as it reaches the end of its range.

The rule then goes on to say that:

- During hour 1: the tide will rise or fall for one twelfth of its range.
- During hour 2: the tide will rise or fall two twelfths of its range.
- During hour 3: the tide will rise or fall three twelfths of its range.
- During hour 4: the tide will rise or fall three twelfths of its range.
- During hour 5: the tide will rise or fall two twelfths of its range.
- During hour 6: the tide will rise or fall for one twelfth of its range.

For a flooding 6m tide, this would mean the water would rise by:

- Hour 1: 0.5m
- Hour 2: 1.0m
- Hour 3: 1.5m
- Hour 4: 1.5m
- Hour 5: 1.0m
- Hour 6: 0.5m

Naturally, the tidal stream will be at its strongest during hours 3 and 4. This rule only works for areas that have regular tides. In places where the tide is irregular – like the central southern coast of the UK – it isn't really helpful.

Passage planning

All skippers have a duty to plan their trip in advance though this doesn't have to be too elaborate. The Marine and Coastguard Agency's (MCA) guidelines say that for "small craft and pleasure vessels, the degree of voyage planning will be dependent on the size of the vessel, its crew and the length of the voyage".

This simply means that a skipper shouldn't just whiz out of a harbour without a thought, but should take a little time first to plan his passage with regard to the tides, weather conditions and any hazards he might meet en route. This could be nothing more than jotting down the time of HW and LW, and perhaps noting a few details on the chart.

Just common sense, really.

ELECTRONIC INSTRUMENTS

This is a huge and fast moving subject that deserves more space than can be allotted in this book. Technological developments have driven down costs to the point where small craft can now carry the sort of electronic gear that would been considered a navigational luxury even on merchant ships just a few decades ago. And there will be more marvels to come, for sure.

Global Positioning System (GPS)

GPS is by no means the first electronic navigational system the world has seen. Ground based Loran and Decca both emerged during World War II and the first satellite system became operational in the 1960s.

All have disappeared in favour of GPS which was originally intended for the US military. It relies on a minimum of at least twenty-four operational satellites orbiting about 20,000 metres above the Earth's surface. Each satellite transmits a signal giving its position and the exact time. The receiver on your boat measures the time delays between transmission and reception and uses the information to compute your position. When you think that the radio signals travel at nearly 300 million metres per second, it's easy to appreciate how incredibly small these delays are, and how astonishing are the devices that process the data.

GPS functions

Even the most basic GPS units will do far more than display your latitude and longitude. Indeed, to understand all their functions typically takes a manual about the size of this book – a manual, incidentally, which should be read, since it contains important information. But there are some common tasks that we should deal with here.

Speed over the ground (SOG) This can differ from speed through the water because the latter may be affected by tidal stream. SOG is the actual progress you are making.

Course over the ground (COG) Otherwise known as your ground track, or Course Made Good (CMG). This is often different from your compass course which may be allowing for the stream. COG is the actual direction in which you're progressing.

Waypoints A waypoint is a position you want to head towards. It may be your final destination or it could be a point where you intend to change course – say, a course alteration off a headland. For anglers, it's often handy to place waypoints over tasty shoals or wrecks. Waypoints can usually be named and stored in your GPS. Also, they can often be strung together as 'routes' and, in many cases, 'reverse routes', so you can follow the same track there and back. Many GPS sets have a 'Go To' button which will give you the course and distance to a waypoint of your choice. Then, as you head towards it, they are able to show Cross Track Error (XTE) if you stray off the ground track.

Understanding datums

You might think that the concept of latitude and longitude would be uniform – that's to say that a position on one chart would precisely match the same position on another. Regrettably, this isn't always so. Because our planet isn't a true sphere, nor spins on a fixed axis, a variety of reference points – datums, as they're called – have been established over the years. Efforts to establish a universal datum still continue, and 1984 saw the arrival of WGS84 (WGS stands for World Geodetic System) which is the standard datum used by GPS and most modern charts.

Until quite recently, British charts were based on Ordnance Survey Great Britain 1936 (OSGB36) and northern European charts to European Datum 1950 (ED50) and there are still a lot of these about. The difference between datums isn't huge on a global scale – in some areas 150m or so – but that could be significant if you wanted to be more precise. For instance, if there was a wreck you wanted to fish on and you took its position from a paper chart and entered it as a waypoint, your GPS might direct you to somewhere close but not spot on. The good news is that GPS sets can be programmed to work to any known datum, but it's important to check that your charts and GPS agree.

Before we leave this subject, it's worth noting that charts aren't always 100% reliable. Many of the surveys were done decades or even centuries ago and have yet to be updated. The fact is that GPS is revealing all sorts of inaccuracies, particularly in remote locations where there's little or no commercial pressure to resurvey.

ELECTRONIC CARTOGRAPHY

It was inevitable that electronic charts would eventually challenge the traditional role of paper ones. When they first appeared they were very expensive but this is another market where street prices have fallen dramatically.

When combined with a GPS you can not only see where you are at any time, but also where you've been, since your progress leaves a sort of snail trail behind it.

Cartography is the art and science of map-making and in the electronic form there are two distinct types:

Raster These are scanned from paper charts and therefore have much the same look about them. Since scanning is a fast and uncomplicated process, raster charts are relatively cheap to produce but they are heavy users of computer memory – though this has become less important when handled by the larger memories of modern computers.

And there are some limitations. Because the image is a copy of a paper chart, corrections can only be made after an updated chart is issued.

Vector The production of vector charts is a painstaking business. It involves plotting each feature – for instance, the coastline and depth contours – as a series of dots that will later be joined up by a computer to form visible lines. The information originally came from conventional cartography but the plotting process digitises the data directly into a computer file. Because only the dots, rather than the complete lines, are recorded, vector charts need much less memory.

An important plus for the vector type is that information can be stored on different layers, which can either be switched on or off at will or will do so automatically as you zoom in and out. This means, for example, that such features as inshore depth soundings or buoys won't clutter the screen when zoomed out, but will suddenly appear when you zoom in. Also, 'interrogation' is possible. This means that when you move the cursor over a feature a window will open to tell you more about it.

Correction of vector charts can be done simply by changing the computer data – a relatively easy task.

Chart plotting hardware

The choice is between running your electronic charts on a laptop computer or on a dedicated chart plotter. Both offer advantages, but most angling boat skippers would choose the latter since marine chart plotters (as opposed to the car type which are very similar) are almost invariably weatherproof.

But there's little doubt which way the technology is leading us. The expectation is that boats will have a multi-purpose console (or consoles) that will display all important information: charts, radar, speed, depth, fish finding, water temperature, oil pressure and so on. And that's not a prediction – the equipment is here today and is likely to become more and more affordable as the years roll by.

It would be difficult to carry as many paper charts as a chart plotter will hold

RADAR

The powerful tool that helped us win the Battle of Britain continues to keep us safe today – but only if it's used properly. There's more than a grain of truth in the old joke about 'radar assisted collisions', where the information was interpreted wrongly. The main problem is that there's a tendency to rely on radar too completely, without fully understanding its limitations.

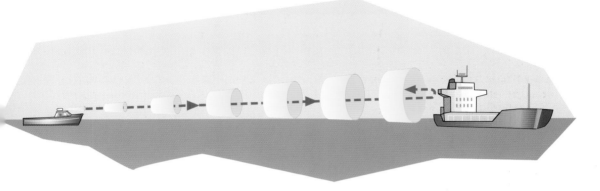

How radar works

The principles behind radar (the word comes from **RA**dio **D**etection **A**nd **R**anging) are well known. A transmitter emits pulses of radio microwaves from a rotating scanner that focuses the beam both horizontally and vertically, rather like sweeping the horizon with a pair of binoculars. If the pulses hit a solid object within range, they are reflected back to the radar's receiver. The time delay between transmission and reception is used to calculate the object's distance, while the rotational position of the scanner tells in what direction it lies.

The radar picture is displayed on a screen, usually with your boat in the centre (though many modern radars allow offset displays). The most common display format is known as 'head-up', as if your bow was pointing towards the top of the screen. In this format, a target on the right-hand side of the screen would be on your starboard side, and one on the left would be to port. With input from an electronic compass, many offer 'north-up' – as if you were seeing the situation on a chart with north at the top – and even 'course-up' where your intended course is at the top. For collision avoidance, most mariners use head-up or course-up because what you see on the screen helps you visualise what's going on around you.

Beam width

Probably the most important part of a radar system is the scanner. Small scanners sell well because they're lighter and cheaper than large ones, but they come with serious limitations. A large scanner will focus the transmission beam width more narrowly, which enables it to pick out smaller details with greater precision. This is because the radar becomes aware of a target as soon as the beam starts to move over it, and continues to do so until it sweeps completely clear. For the whole time the target is somewhere within the beam, an echo will be returned. In Fig 9.6 a tiny target will appear much bigger on the screen and the gap in the sea wall won't be noticed at all. On the other hand the narrower beam (Fig 9:7) will show the gap clearly.

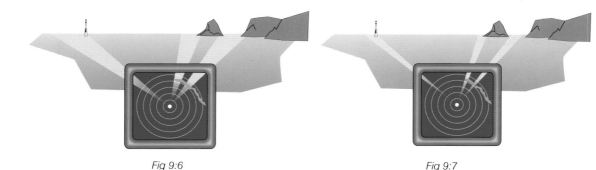

Fig 9:6   Fig 9:7

Bearings and range

Virtually all radars come with an Electronic Bearing Line (EBL) facility. The EBL is a line – usually dotted – that radiates out from your position on the screen and can be rotated to lie over a target to obtain a bearing. When in head-up or course-up modes the bearing will be relative to your heading and must be corrected, as shown below, to produce a compass bearing.

The Variable Range Marker (VRM) does a similar job for range. The VRM is a circle – again centred on your boat – that can be expanded and contracted to measure distances away. Unlike bearings, which suffer the distorting effects of beam width, you can consider the range to be accurate whatever the size of the scanner. However, you do need to know what you're looking at. A boat running parallel to the coast in thick fog ran aground because the echoes he thought were the shoreline turned out to be blocks of flats set many metres inland.

Position by range and bearing

A good way to plot your position on a chart is to use EBL and VRM together.

- Select a target that can be positively identified (such as a buoy or distinct headland) and lay the EBL over it. Make an allowance for beam width if you think it necessary.

- Convert the relative bearing into a true one.

- Obtain the range with the VRM.

- Reproduce the two on your chart.

Range and bearing is a simple way of finding your position

Echo sounders and fishfinders

Few sea anglers will need an introduction to fishfinders – those marvellous developments of depth sounders that both trace the undulations of the sea bed and also reveal what potential catches might be lurking in the depths.

Echo sounders – often called depth sounders – and fishfinders work on the same principle. A sound pulse is emitted by a 'transducer'. The sound echo bounces back from the bottom (or fish) and the time delay is used to compute the depth. This is similar to the way radar works but, of course, with sound waves rather than microwaves. Echo sounders use either rotating LEDs or have digital displays. Fishfinders plot successive soundings as a continuous, rolling representation – a sort of brief history of what went on below you. A fishfinder display might be in black and white or colour – the coloured one being by far the easiest to interpret.

Belt and braces navigation

Navigators should be prepared to use all the tools at their disposal. The arrival of GPS and radar has had the unfortunate effect of making some of us neglect more conventional methods.

For example, running along a well defined depth contour – or between two depth contours – is a good way of working your way along a coast in poor visibility. Of course, since the contours marked on the chart are effectively for the lowest possible tide (apart from in exceptional circumstances), you have to allow for the tidal height at that time. Handily, many chart plotters will display tidal information. Or you may choose to use The Rule of Twelfths (see page 69).

In the days before there were any fancy instruments, navigators employed all manner of odd tricks – one of them interestingly predicting echo sounders and radars. When closing a cliff-lined shore in fog they used a loud noise (a shout, a whistle or even a musket shot) and counted the seconds before the echo returned. Sound travels at about 377yds (340m) per second and you have to allow for it to go there and back. Another useful guide is that, with your eyes just 5ft (1,52m) above the waterline, if you can just see the breakers at the foot of a cliff, then that cliff is about 2.5nm away. Not exactly rocket science but – who knows? – it might come in useful one day…

Unmarked rivers

It's not unusual for creeks and rivers either to have very few navigation marks or none whatsoever. Even marks that might be found are often simple withies – sticks stuck in the mud, here today gone tomorrow.

Luckily for us, rivers are fairly predictable. Along the straighter reaches the faster, deeper water tends to be in the middle. On bends the centrifugal force throws the stream outwards, carving out the bottom where it runs. So the general rules are:

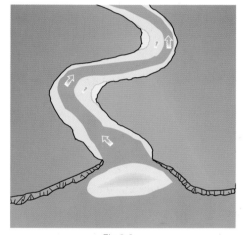

Fig 9:8

■ Stick to the centre where the river runs straight. Keep to the outside where it bends. The inside of bends can be very shallow indeed (Fig 9:8).

■ Be watchful for rocks on the banks – they could extend out into the river.

■ Rivers often have bars at their entrance. Be very careful entering, especially with an onshore wind.

■ If you're a small vessel, don't forget your obligations under Colreg rule 9(b). You must not impede another vessel which can only navigate in the deeper channel.

NOTE: Whether navigating conventionally or by electronics, there's much more to navigation than could ever be covered here. Anyone wanting to learn more is urged to read the RYA Navigation Handbook which covers the subject in far greater depth.

Chapter 10

WIND AND WAVES

GLOBAL WEATHER

The force that drives the Earth's weather patterns is the heat from the Sun. Basically, the air in the hot equatorial regions rises and spreads north and south towards the poles. But the flow isn't smooth. Various factors create irregularities: the alternate heating and cooling effects of night and day; the inconsistent scatter of the various land masses; the fact that land warms and cools rapidly, while sea temperatures change slowly; and, of course, there's the tilting of the Earth's axis that brings summer and winter.

All of which makes for quite a chaotic situation that's notoriously difficult to forecast. But there are some facts we can state with certainty:

- The air in areas of low atmospheric pressure is rising and in high pressure areas it's falling.

- The surface air flows from high pressure towards low pressure, spiralling outwards from highs and inwards into lows.

But the air doesn't move in straight lines. The Earth's spin (towards the east) causes both low and high pressure systems to circulate – and always in predictable directions.

- Northern hemisphere winds circulate clockwise around high pressure and anticlockwise around low pressure. If you stand facing the wind, the lowest pressure lies to your right.

- Southern hemisphere winds circulate anticlockwise around high pressure and clockwise around low pressure. When facing the wind, the lowest pressure lies to your left.

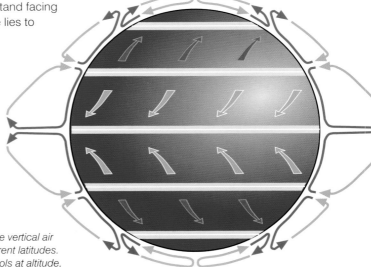

Fig 10:1 shows the vertical air circulations at different latitudes. The hot air rises, cools at altitude, and then descends to start the cycle again.

DEPRESSIONS

For those of us who inhabit the mid to higher latitudes, few things make us groan so loudly as news that another depression is on its way. For mariners, these are particularly bad tidings for we know to expect strong winds, rough seas and lots of rain.

So, how are they born? Well, in the higher latitudes the simple answer is to say that the fault lies with the polar fronts, but the subject deserves a fuller explanation.

If viewed from the side, the Earth's weather system (greatly simplified) would be seen as being divided into bands that are mirrored each side of the equator – or more accurately, north and south of the Intertropical Convergence Zone (ITCZ), more commonly known as the doldrums. The ITCZ is a band of low pressure where the northern and southern weather systems meet.

You will see from Fig 10:1 that both poles are capped with areas of high pressure. These are the 'polar highs' and their boundaries are known as 'polar fronts'. The air in the polar highs is relatively dry and cold, unlike in the neighbouring regions where it's warm and moist, having been originally drawn up from the tropics. Note how the winds oppose each other along the polar fronts.

The development of a depression is shown in Fig 10:2.

This sequence shows the development and collapse of a depression in the northern hemisphere. The same occurs along the south polar front, but those latitudes are largely uninhabited. When you consider that the southern Australian city of Melbourne is about the same distance from the equator as is Alicante in Spain, the picture becomes clear. So, from here on, when referring to depressions it's the north we're talking about.

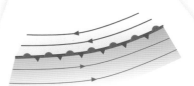

1. The cold air and warm air lie peacefully alongside each other

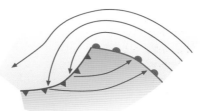

2. An atmospheric disturbance creates a kink in the polar front

3. The opposing winds and differences in pressure bring a rotational force and the wind starts to circulate within the depression, with cold and warm fronts leading the air masses they represent. That's to say, the warm front is the forward edge of the warm air and the cold front is the same for the cold.

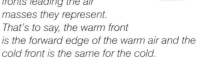

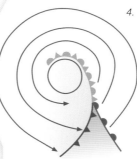

4. Eventually, the cold front catches up with the warm front and they become one – the technical term is 'occluded'. Although the depression is on its last legs, this final stage usually produces a band of heavy rain.

Fig 10:2

Depressions – what to expect

Of course, it's the practical effects we have to cope with. First let's deal with the words 'veering' and 'backing' which refer to changes in wind direction.

■ Veering is when the wind direction changes in a clockwise shift – for instance, west towards north.

■ Backing is when the wind direction shifts anti-clockwise – for instance, west to south.

Naturally, most of us rely on weather forecasts to warn us of approaching bad weather, but it's still handy to be aware of visual signs that things are turning nasty. Since the majority of depressions pass to north of most of us, let's assume this is the case here. Early indications include:

■ High, wispy white (cirrus) clouds, commonly called 'mares' tails'. They often have hooked ends.

■ The wind backs towards the south.

■ The barometer (if you have one) starts to fall.

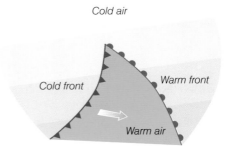

Fig 10:3

Unless you are far offshore, these indicators should give you plenty of time to head for shelter, but if you do get caught out, this is what you can expect in the various sectors of a depression as it passes over you.

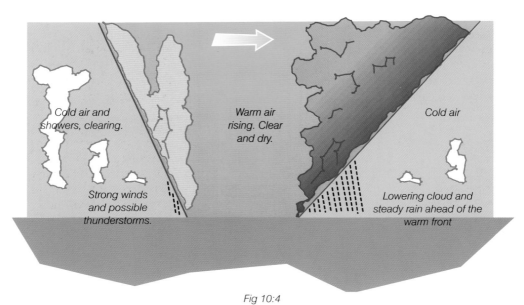

Fig 10:4

Anticyclones

These areas of high pressure usually travel less rapidly than depressions – indeed, some (such as the Azores high) are semi-permanent, though they are by no means totally stationary, nor of constant atmospheric pressure.

Within an anticyclone you can expect fine weather with steady, generally light winds, getting calmer towards the centre. Highs can also give rise to coastal fogs, particularly in the morning before the sun burns them off.

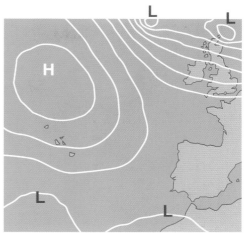

Fig 10:5

Sea breezes and land breezes

Weather doesn't always develop on a huge scale. Local effects can be surprisingly powerful. Sea and land breezes are opposite sides of the same coin. Both arise from the fact that land heats and cools rapidly while the sea maintains a steadier temperature.

The sea breeze (Fig 10:6) is caused by the land heating under sunlight. The hot air rises upwards and, in doing so, sucks cooler air in from over the sea. The result is an onshore breeze that can extend to about 20nm offshore. Although in Britain

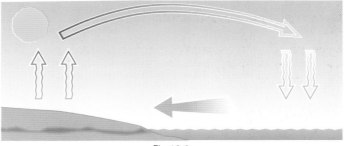

Fig 10:6

sea breezes are usually fairly moderate, in hotter climates – particularly along mountainous coasts – they can reach gale force. As evening comes and the land cools, sea breezes die away…

…sometimes to be replaced by a land breeze (Fig 10:7). Here the convection process becomes reversed once the land becomes cooler than the sea – that's to say the warm air rises from the water, drawing cool air from the land. This is usually a pretty feeble phenomenon although it can be reinforced on hilly coasts where falling air slides outwards over the sea, rather like a skier on the slopes.

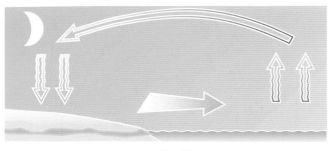

Fig 10:7

Fig 10:8

Thunderstorms

These potentially dangerous monsters are also driven by heat convection, and can be recognised by the towering (cumulonimbus) clouds that can reach up to 12km high into the sky. Thunderclouds often have anvil shaped heads, caused by the jet stream tugging the cloud top to one side.

There are various types of thunderstorm, but they all work by a similar mechanism: hot air is carried upwards by convection, then descends with great force after it cools at high altitude. Depending on the temperatures, you're very likely to get heavy rain or hail.

Since they're fuelled by heat, thunderstorms in Britain are a fairly rare feature of the summer months. In hotter climates they're to be found year-round and are a lot more destructive. The thunder itself is caused by lightning, with the time lag between the flash and the thunderclap being due to the difference between the speed of light and the much slower speed of sound – about six seconds per mile. Actually, this gives you a useful tool. By timing the delay in seconds and dividing it by six, you can estimate how far away the thunderstorm is. If the delays gets shorter, you know it's getting closer.

FOG

There are few meteorological phenomena mariners dread more than fog. With the arrival of radar and GPS, the threats may have diminished but they certainly haven't disappeared. The skipper of a small boat may hear the throb of a large ship or see a strong echo on his radar screen, but has the ship seen him? Almost anyone will feel vulnerable. We shall be looking at safety tactics in the next chapter but for now let's investigate how fogs form.

Advection fog

Fogs are nothing more than very low clouds and are made up of minute water droplets suspended in the air. For mariners, the most common type is 'advection fog' (Fig 10:9). This is formed when the wind blows warm, moist air over a colder surface where it condenses. Coastal fog and sea

Fig 10:9

fog are both advection fogs and can only occur when the wind speed is below about 15 knots. Higher wind speeds will lift the fog to form low cloud.

Valley Fog

Although more commonly an inland feature, valley fog can cause problems within hill flanked estuaries. At night the air cools and becomes denser, sliding down the hillsides into the valley. If the temperature of the valley floor – water in an estuary – is cold enough, condensation occurs and fog is formed. Since estuaries are often sheltered from the wind, the fog may linger even when it's perfectly clear outside.

Fog tactics

There are few occasions where you feel more helpless than when caught out in fog. And with reason, since this is undeniably a dangerous situation. The Colregs tell us that 'every vessel shall proceed at a safe speed adapted to the prevailing circumstances and condition of restricted visibility' – identical advice to that given to drivers when fog blankets our roads ashore. Unfortunately, as we know from the casualty figures, not everybody heeds the warnings.

So, you can never be entirely safe; but there are steps we can take to minimise the risks. Here are a few tips.

- Comply with the Regulations yourself. Keep your speed low and sound a single prolonged (meaning between 4 and 6 seconds) blast on a foghorn every two minutes.

- Keep a constant lookout and listen intently. Call a halt to meaningless chatter and – if under power – every few minutes throttle back (or even stop) the engine so you have periods of near silence to listen for other sound signals or engines.

- Carry a radar reflector and make sure it's mounted correctly. Speeding vessels will almost certainly be relying on their radars, so you need to present as strong an echo as possible.

- If at all possible, avoid shipping routes – particularly traffic separation schemes where ships are funnelled into narrow lanes. If you really must cross, do so at 90° and be very, very careful. If you have VHF, it's not a bad idea to put out a SECURITÉ (pronounced 'say-cure-it-ay') message, informing other vessels of your position (either in lat and long or, better still, relative to a known landmark – for instance, 'ten miles southwest of Bluster Point'). Also give a brief description of your boat plus its speed and intended course. You may even get a helpful response from a ship who has spotted you on his radar, advising whether or not it appears safe to cross. (Note: Emergency VHF procedures are described on page 84. To learn more about VHF you should refer to the RYA VHF Handbook.)

- You can hide from the big stuff by working your way into shallow water, perhaps anchoring until the fog clears. Of course, you must be careful to avoid any inshore hazards.

Chapter 11

WHEN THE GOING GETS ROUGH

The phrase 'heavy weather' means different things to different people. Whereas a lively Force 6 would mean nothing to passengers aboard an ocean liner, it could be very uncomfortable for anglers caught out in unprotected waters.

The first rule of seamanship is to avoid exposing yourself to danger in the first place. Modern weather forecasting has become so reliable that it could be claimed that anyone caught out in a

blow has only himself to blame. But that would be unfair. Although it's easy enough to predict the arrival of meteorological disturbances, it's not so easy to anticipate their strength. Force 7 winds were forecast for the 1979 Fastnet yacht race but no one expected the hurricane Force 11 that hammered the fleet and so tragically took the lives of 15 sailors. The truth is that the weather can play tricks on us, and we need to be prepared.

It is important to understand that it's not usually the winds themselves that cause problems – it's the waves they stir up. Far offshore the waves are entirely wind-created, but in coastal waters there are a number of other factors at work. These include:

- The strength and direction of the tidal stream. If the tide runs against the wind – that's to say in the opposite direction – it will be very much rougher than if they were both going more or less the same way. 'Wind against stream' is bad news. 'Wind over stream' is much better.

- And, of course, there's the nature of the seabed. Underwater obstructions can cause 'upwellings', piling up the seas in confused and sometimes dangerous patches.

- Then there are 'tidal races' which occur in constricted channels or where the seabed becomes shallow off prominent headlands. The stream accelerates and the waves become steeper and higher. In the worst conditions you can expect overfalls and even whirlpools. Nasty.

- The shape of the coastline can leave you exposed or protected. The 'windward' side facing the full brunt of wind and waves will be rough while the 'leeward' side will be far more tranquil. Sheltering in the lee of the land is a time honoured seamanship practice.

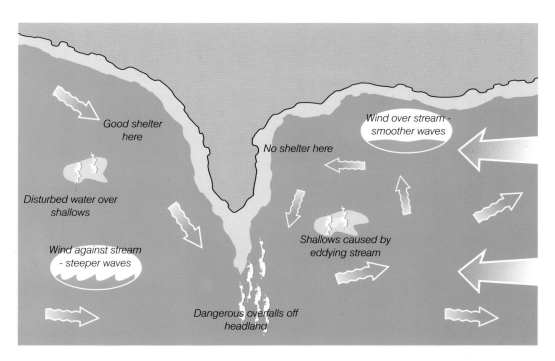

Sea conditions can vary greatly from place to place

Working with the waves

Waves are produced by the friction between the wind and water. At first glance it might seem as if the whole surface of the sea is moving bodily downwind, but this is not the case. Except for currents and other streams, the water is pretty much stationary – at least in the horizontal plane, though there can be plenty of vertical movement.

'Fetch' is the distance the wind moves over the water. The greater the fetch,
the rougher the water will be.

But there is more going on inside each wave than the water simply rising and falling. There is also an orbital, wheel-like movement which can best be understood by imagining a single water molecule on the surface. As each wave passes, that molecule will be carried round in an almost perfect circle, ending up almost exactly where it was before. This means that the surface flow runs in different directions depending on where you are on the wave face – an important issue when it comes to handling a boat in tough conditions.

Not all boats handle in precisely the same manner, but here's some general guidance.

Motoring downwind

It might seem illogical but 'following seas' – meaning waves approaching from astern – present one of the most dangerous circumstances for small craft. This is because the wave's surface flow will propel you off the crest and then rush up to meet you in the trough. The result can be to spin the boat around so it ends up broadside to the waves. This is known as 'broaching' and can easily lead to capsize.

Very careful use of the throttle is called for. Ease it back as you approach each crest, then accelerate as you enter the trough to give you the power and steerageway needed to climb the next wave. Better still, choose a calmer moment to turn round and head upwind to another source of shelter. Avoid beam seas if at all possible.

The bow digs in ... the rotational forces in the wave cause a broach ... and a boat can be rolled

Motoring upwind

Uncomfortable, but safer. Now the wave crest's surface flow will slow you down and increase steerageway. Ease off a little as you punch through the crest, then accelerate down the back of the wave ready for the next one.

It's often easier to steer a zigzag course at about 30°–40° to the wind. This has the effect of lengthening the distance between crests, thereby giving you more time to adjust your speed.

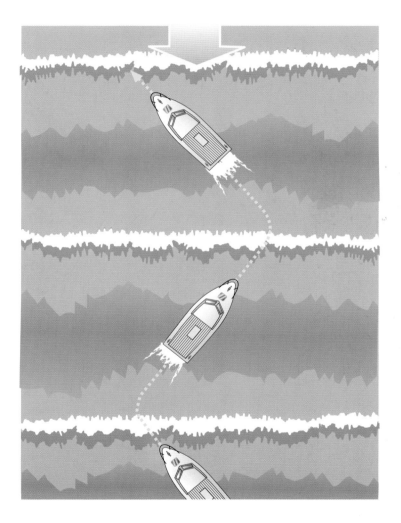

IMPORTANT!! Try and keep as warm and dry as possible. The combination of wet clothing and wind chill can seriously reduce both morale and efficiency. And, if all on board are not wearing them already, you should dig out the lifejackets.

Chapter 12

EMERGENCIES

An emergency is any incident where there's a potential threat to life. Sometimes that threat will be obvious – fire, sinking, a man overboard (MOB) or one who has suffered serious injury – and sometimes it involves problems you believe you can handle – engine breakdown, a manageable leak, perhaps a rope around the prop. Whether you need assistance or not often comes down to the judgement of the skipper but it's always better to think the worst and let others know of your problems. If in doubt DON'T HESITATE!

USING VHF

The direst emergencies are defined as being 'when a vessel or person is in grave and imminent danger and requires immediate assistance'. This demands a MAYDAY call. First select Channel 16, then proceed as follows:

MAYDAY, MAYDAY, MAYDAY

THIS IS MOTOR BOAT
(say boat's name three times)

MAYDAY
(say boat's name once)

MY POSITION IS
(give lat & long or true bearing and distance from a charted point)

(Give MMSI if your radio has DSC)

WE ARE (on fire, sinking whatever) **AND REQUIRE IMMEDIATE ASSISTANCE**

SIX (or however many) **PERSONS ON BOARD**

OVER

PAN PAN

For lesser emergencies, when there is no immediate danger but you do need assistance you should make a PAN PAN call like this:

PAN PAN, PAN PAN, PAN PAN

ALL SHIPS, ALL SHIPS, ALL SHIPS

THIS IS MOTOR BOAT
(say boat's name repeated three times)

MY POSITION IS
(lat & long or true bearing and distance from a charted point)

(Give MMSI if you have DSC)

I HAVE LOST MY RUDDER (or whatever) **AND REQUIRE A TOW**

SIX (or however many) **PERSONS ON BOARD**

OVER

Digital Selective Calling (DSC)

Not all VHF sets have DSC, but those that do can automatically transmit information on your plight by simply pressing a button. The message will include your MMSI code so the rescue services will know who you are and what sort of vessel is in distress. If connected to GPS it will also give your position.

OTHER DISTRESS SIGNALS

- Flames on the vessel (as from a burning oil or tar barrel!)
- A gun or other explosive device fired at approximately one minute intervals.

Orange smoke device

Red flares – either hand held or parachute type

A continuous sounding of any fog signalling device

The international code flags NC

Repeatedly raising and lowering outstretched arms

A square flag with a ball (or anything resembling a ball) above or below it.

Sending the morse code group SOS by any means

MAN OVERBOARD (MOB)

Even in good conditions this is a very serious incident. In rough weather or at night it becomes very grave indeed. If it isn't to become a tragedy, those left on board must act promptly and efficiently.

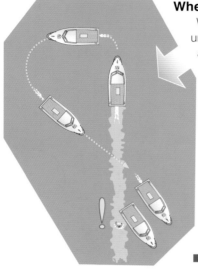

When you see him go

With all the cockpit activity typical on an angling boat, it's unlikely that someone should fall overboard unseen. So let's assume that at least one other person saw him go. What then?

■ Alert all on board by shouting 'man overboard'.

■ One person should be told to keep the MOB in sight at all times. He should point in his direction.

■ Throw a lifebuoy (preferably a danbuoy type with a whip mast, flag and light) or any other large buoyant object (perhaps a fender) overboard to mark the spot.

■ At slow speeds, the helmsman should turn towards the MOB to throw the stern and prop away from him. At higher speeds the MOB will be well astern before there is time to do this.

■ Make a slow turn to go back and recover the MOB.

■ This is a MAYDAY situation, either by voice or DSC. Don't hesitate. After a successful recovery you can cancel the alert.

Fig 12:1

In darkness or poor visibility

In these unenviable circumstances it may be impossible to keep the MOB in sight, so you must use a manoeuvre that should bring you back onto your own wake.

■ As soon as the MOB cry goes up, the helmsman should note the compass heading and, if the compass allows, the reciprocal course – that's to say, the heading 180° to your original.

■ Then quickly alter course 60° either way. This gives you space to turn …

■ … by putting the helm hard over the other way until you come round to your reciprocal course, which you should continue down until you find your MOB.

■ Again, don't forget the MAYDAY call. In such circumstances, it's even more likely that you will need outside assistance.

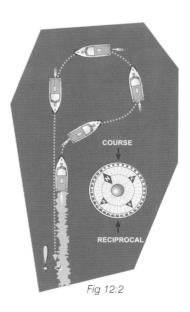

COURSE

RECIPROCAL

Fig 12:2

Search pattern

If you fail to find the MOB you must search for him – and do so methodically. The best method is to conduct what's known as an 'expanding box search'. Here's how to go about it.

- Drop a floating marker nearest to the point where you think the MOB might be. This will be your 'datum point', the start of your search pattern.

- To keep matters as simple as possible, motor in a northerly direction until you can still just see the datum point, the distance you have motored we shall call 'D', meaning 'detection range'. If the boat has no means of measuring distance, it might be helpful to note the time it took and use this as your reference.

- Then turn right and motor the same distance (or time) in an easterly direction.

- Then turn south. You will see from the diagram that the length of the leg increases by one D every two legs – thereby expanding the box. Continue until you locate the MOB.

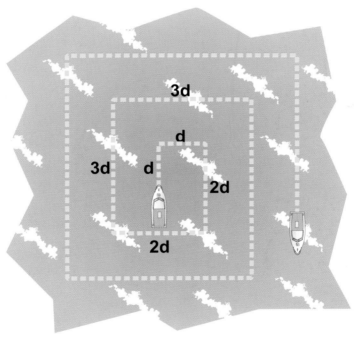

Fig 12:3

Effects of stream and wind

Because both the MOB and your search pattern will be drifting with the stream, you should make no allowance for it. However, boats with high superstructures may need to allow for the effects of the wind, which will affect them much more than the MOB.

Most GPS sets have an MOB button which records the position and gives the course and distance back. You must remember that this is the position over the ground and that the MOB will be carried downstream and could be some distance away by the time you return.

Recovering the MOB

Many boats have their lowest freeboard aft so this is usually the easiest and safest place to get your MOB on board again. Don't try and approach him by going astern – he could be injured by the prop. There are two recommended methods.

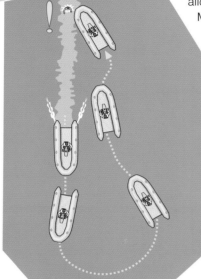

Fig 12:4

Upwind approach

This is the preferred technique in rougher conditions, since it allows you to meet the seas head-on and there's little risk of the MOB being drawn under the boat (See Fig 12:4).

■ Make sure all fishing lines are out of the water. The MOB has had a tough enough time already without becoming someone's catch.

■ Give yourself room to manoeuvre and approach slowly from downwind, using forward and neutral to adjust your speed.

■ When close enough, turn to one side so he is just off the bow, select neutral and either throw him a line or grab him. He may be both cold and exhausted so don't expect him to fend for himself.

Beam on approach

A good technique for calmer conditions

■ Motor to a position directly upwind of the MOB, keeping the wind on your beam.

■Once in place, select neutral and drift down onto the MOB (See Fig 12:1). Once he's alongside, switch off the engine.

First aid for the MOB

Get him out of his wet clothes and wrap him in coats or a blanket. If he's alert a warm non-alcoholic drink will help him recover. But if you suspect he is suffering from hypothermia (symptoms: slurred speech, very pale skin, abnormally slow breathing and extreme lethargy) seek immediate medical advice via VHF. The first half hour after rescue is a critical period. The SAR (Search and Rescue) services may want to bring him ashore as quickly as possible.

Practise, practise, practise!

Don't wait until you need them. Practise these techniques in advance, using a fender as a dummy casualty. And take the crew by surprise. A wise skipper will periodically spring a faked MOB on his crew when they least expect it.

FLOODING

Unless your boat has suffered catastrophic damage through collision or grounding, the most common cause of flooding is a split or burst hose – often part of the engine cooling water system. Other causes could be a leaking stern gland (where the prop shaft exits the hull) or failure of a seacock or through-hull fitting. Either way, the source of your troubles should be quite easy to trace.

An important check is to taste the water. If it's fresh or only a little salty you can breathe a sigh of relief because it's probable that the water tank or its hoses have let go. You may have to go without your afternoon cuppa but there's clearly no danger.

But if it's seawater the situation is more serious. Your actions at this point depend on the severity of the problem. It's been said that the most efficient bilge pump is a frightened man with a bucket, but obviously, if the water is gaining on you and there's no immediate help around, a MAYDAY call is justified. However, if you believe you can fix it but the boat is disabled then a PAN PAN will suffice to obtain a tow. While considering your options you should remember that electric bilge pumps draw power from the batteries and these in turn depend on the engine to keep them charged. No engine means limited life for the batteries.

TIP A useful item to have on board is a roll of self-amalgamating tape, which can often be used to make temporary repairs to hoses.

FIRE

There are few experiences more terrifying than a fire at sea. Although not very common, when they occur there's almost always a potential threat to life. Unfortunately, motor boats tend to be stuffed with inflammable substances: fuel for the engine, oils or paints, perhaps gas for the cooker and so on. Subjected to enough heat, even the resin in glassfibre mouldings will burn – down to the waterline in many instances. In such circumstances, remaining on board becomes impossible. The only course is to abandon ship.

For a fire to exist, it needs three things: fuel, oxygen and a heat source. This dangerous trio is known as the 'fire triangle' and if you take away any one of those elements the fire will go out. Since it's not always practical to remove the fuel, most fire fighting methods concentrate on quenching the heat and starving the fire of oxygen, sometimes both at once.

A fire can be triggered by a number of means, but electrical malfunctions top the list. It's a sad fact that boat electrical systems are not always as sound as they should be, with many having been adapted or extended by well-meaning owners over the years. A widespread belief is that 12V systems are inherently safe, but it's not always appreciated that, for any given electrical load, low voltage means high amperage – and it's amps that cause wires to overheat.

What extinguisher and when

There are various types of fire extinguisher which can be broadly classified by the chemical – known as the 'extinguishant' – they contain. For the mariner the most plentiful source of extinguishant is the water over the side, and for some fires it will serve very well. However, for electrical fires it is worse than useless and, if thrown on burning oil, it could actually spread the fire and make matters worse.

So, it has to be appreciated that not all extinguishers will be effective in every situation. It's important to know what type to use.

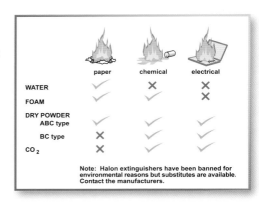

	paper	chemical	electrical
WATER	✓	✗	✗
FOAM	✓	✓	✗
DRY POWDER ABC type	✓	✓	✓
BC type	✗	✓	✓
CO_2	✗	✓	✓

Note: Halon extinguishers have been banned for environmental reasons but substitutes are available. Contact the manufacturers.

Fig 12:5

Engine fires

■ Remember the fire triangle and do not open the engine box. To admit more air could turn a smouldering fire into a blazing inferno.

■ Turn off the fuel.

■ Switch off engine electrics. Hopefully this will be on its own circuit because if the situation deteriorates you may soon need power to make a MAYDAY or PAN PAN call.

■ Ideally, all engine compartments should contain an automatic or remote control extinguisher. If not they should have a small access port through which a hand-held extinguisher can be discharged (Fig 12:5).

Galley fires

■ Turn off the gas or other fuel.

■ Never douse the flames with water. Burning fat will be thrown everywhere and you could be badly scalded.

■ Instead, the best action is to smother the fire with a fire blanket. Protect your hands by keeping them on the safe side of the blanket as you do so.

Clothes on fire

■ Another job for the fire blanket. If the casualty is standing, get him to lie down and roll over. Wrap the fire blanket around him. If it's your clothes that are burning, grab the fire blanket and do the same.

■ Once the fire is out, rinse any burned areas with copious amounts of water to cool them down. Don't attempt to peel off charred clothing. Use the VHF to seek medical advice immediately.

> ### General guidelines
>
> - Aim extinguishers towards the base of the fire.
>
> - It's better to splash or spray water than it is to throw it on as a deluge. Spraying increases the cooling effect. However, a bucketful is much better than nothing. **Remember: not on oil or electrical fires!**
>
> - If possible, turn the boat downwind. This reduces the apparent wind speed and thereby the fanning effect. It also means the flames will be blown forward, away from the cockpit from where you might have to abandon ship.
>
> - Don't hesitate to put out a PAN PAN or MAYDAY call. The Search and Rescue (SAR) services would much prefer to know about your problem early. They can always be stood down if the fire is successfully extinguished.

ABANDONING SHIP

It is sometimes said that the time to abandon ship is when you have to step upwards into the liferaft. This isn't literally true of course, but is a light-hearted way of saying that your boat is where you are safest and you should stay with her until you are absolutely sure it's time to leave. Certainly lives have been lost through abandoning ship too soon. Unmanned boats have been found afloat with the crew and liferaft lost.

Of course, the exception to this admittedly simplistic advice is a fire you can't contain. Since liferafts can easily be damaged by the flames, it's sensible to admit defeat in good time and put yourself at a safe distance from the inferno.

But liferafts are not the only option.

Jump and swim
If other boats have come to your aid they would be foolish to come alongside if you are on fire. However, if they are in close attendance it would be entirely practical for your crew to slip on lifejackets and jump overboard. Choose the windward side to avoid your boat being blown down onto you.

Take to the dinghy
Few angling boats have dinghies but, if one is available, in reasonable conditions this is often the best choice since dinghies are manoeuvrable and liferafts aren't. You may even be able to make your way safely ashore.

Beaching
If the weather and the nature of the coast allows, driving the boat up onto a beach and scrambling ashore might be the best decision. But be very wary if there's a stiff onshore wind. What might seem like harmless waves offshore can become dangerous surf as you approach the shallows. Don't forget to wear lifejackets.

LAUNCHING THE LIFERAFT

All skippers should be familiar with the recommendations for their own specific raft, but this is the general procedure.

- Check that the liferaft's painter is secured to the boat. Make sure the crew are all wearing lifejackets. If available, someone should have grabbed a hand-held VHF and EPIRB.

- Throw the raft into the water from the leeward side so it will drift clear once you have boarded. This may be more then a one-man job – they are surprisingly heavy.

- Pull on the painter until it starts to inflate. Don't be discouraged if this doesn't happen immediately – the painter is longer than you might think.

- Bring the raft close alongside and try to keep as dry as possible while you clamber in. The strongest and most able person should board the raft first so he can assist by hauling his mates in.

- Once all are on board and sitting evenly spaced around the raft, cut the painter. There should be a knife stowed near the entrance for this purpose.

- Stream the drogue you should find inside the raft. This will minimise drift.

- Finally, close the entrance and make yourself as comfortable as possible by bailing out any water. Call the SAR (Search And Rescue) units and advise that you are all now safely in the raft. Hopefully, the EPIRB will have been activated long before now – if not, this wouldn't be a bad time to do it!

Fig 12:6

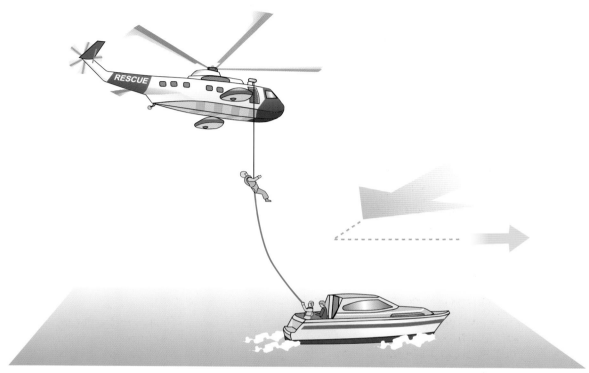

Fig 12:7

HELICOPTER RESCUE

Helicopters are often used to take off single casualties or whole crews. The procedure varies according to the circumstances and it's the pilot's job to decide how to go about it. He will contact you by VHF and it's essential you follow his directions exactly. Take notes if necessary.

■ Smaller boats are usually instructed to remain stationary but you may be asked to maintain a constant course and speed. Do whatever you're told.

■ Make sure the deck is entirely cleared of fishing rods and lines – ideally, a job you should have done before the helicopter arrives. Expect lots of noise and down draught.

■ A weighted line is lowered. This must be allowed to touch the water to discharge any static before you handle it. Do not attach the line to the boat.

■ As the winchman descends, guide him to the boat with the line. A pair of gloves helps. Try not to get the line tangled – coil or flake it, perhaps into a bucket.

■ Once the winchman is on deck he will unhook himself and assess the situation. He is now completely in command so don't waste time arguing. He knows what he's doing.

■ As the casualty and winchman are lifted off the boat, use the weighted line to steady their swing. Make sure it doesn't snag on anything.

LIFEBOAT RESCUE

The role of the lifeboat is to save lives – not to salvage stricken boats. That said, they will often take a boat in tow if the circumstances allow. Indeed, sometimes it's the safest way to bring those in peril back to port.

Having contacted the rescue services, what should you do then?

- Assess your predicament as honestly as you can. If it might be possible to tow your boat home, think how this might be done. As we touched on in the earlier section on towing (page 45) the cleats on many smaller craft are often far too light to take severe loads. You may need to rig a bridle, taking the ropes back to stronger parts of the structure. If the lifeboat does take you in it will be his towline that will be used – almost certainly mightier than anything you might have on board. Also think about protecting against chafe – spare clothing folded into pads serving very well for this task.

- Clear the cockpit of rods, lines and tackle – in fact any objects that might hinder the operation.

- The lifeboat should contact you (if he can) in advance by VHF advising you of his estimated time of arrival (ETA) and asking for further information on your plight – how many on board, are they fit, disabled, injured whatever. Communicate this information to him very clearly.

- Once the lifeboat arrives, the coxswain becomes the 'on scene commander' – to use their own words. Don't argue with anything they do and don't be offended if their manner sounds curt. They won't waste words on idle chitchat and neither should you. However, they will do what they can to put you at ease and it's important for them to know who the skipper is or who has taken over if the skipper is out of action. In short, the lifeboatmen will want to know who to talk to and all others should stay as silent as possible unless there is an important reason to butt in.

- Be prepared to receive lines, following their instructions exactly.

- The lifeboat may put their own crew members on board. Again, don't protest. If an injury is involved, they will assess the severity or otherwise and it may be decided that a helicopter should be called to get him to hospital without delay.

RIB RESCUE

If you are well inshore and the weather is reasonable, you may be attended by an inshore lifeboat, almost always a RIB manned by either 2 or 3 crew members. The general principles are pretty much the same as for the fully crewed offshore lifeboats – with one exception. The towing capabilities of these much lighter craft are greatly reduced, so they are much more likely to take you off and leave your boat to (hopefully) be salvaged by others.

Chapter 13

RUNNING REPAIRS

Mechanical breakdowns are common at sea. The salty environment is harsh on both corrodible mechanisms and electrical systems. Obviously, the best prevention is regular maintenance but even the most lovingly maintained vessel can expect to break down occasionally. For that we should be prepared.

Clearly, not every eventuality for every type of boat and propulsion arrangement can be covered in a few pages, so this chapter deals only with general advice. Different circumstances might demand different provisions.

Tools and spares

It seems a central truth that, no matter how many tools you carry, one day you will come across a problem that calls for something you haven't got. Since it's in the very nature of boats to venture to places where outside assistance is scarce, a wise skipper will prepare for the day when he may have to roll up his sleeves and get himself out of trouble. Of course you can't anticipate every event, but at least you can ensure that when things go wrong you have some basic tools on board. Clearly, the bigger the boat the more comprehensive can be your tool kit. Ultimately, it's for the skipper to decide what he or she needs.

Tool kit

- Engine manual

- Spanners or wrenches. 7mm to 24mm in metric sizes or 1/4in to 1in AF (across flats) if the engine was made in America. Combination spanners have open jaws on one end and 'rings' on the other — both fitting the same size nuts. Spanners with open jaws at both ends are sized differently — e.g. 12mm and 14mm — meaning you only need half the number to cover the whole range.

- Adjustable spanners. These might make a professional cringe but there's no doubt they come in handy — particularly in larger sizes, when they can really be effective.

- Set of Allen keys (wrenches). Yet another choice to be made between metric and imperial, but make sure they're good and long because you often need the leverage.

- Screwdrivers. A comprehensive selection including flat-bladed and cross-point (Phillips and/or Posidrive) in a range of sizes. The short 'dumpy' types are very handy where space is tight.

- Pliers. Conventional and needle-nosed. Also very useful are what are known as 'water pump pliers' or 'crescent wrenches', that can be opened to grip large objects.

- Vice grips — another tool that will bring a shudder to all sensitive souls, but far too versatile and useful not to be included.

- Grease gun and small squirt type oil can

- Multimeter — preferably the digital type which is easier to read with your head down in the engine bay.

- Wire strippers and crimpers, either as separate implements or a multi-purpose tool.

- Hydrometer for testing battery charge — only appropriate if your batteries are liquid lead acid type with accessible cells. If not you will have to rely on your multimeter.

Engine spares

- Oil for engine and gearbox

- Oil filter

- Fuel filters — one spare element or cartridge for each.

- Various greases for pumps, stern glands and general use.

- Penetrating oil in an aerosol can

- Pump impellers — particularly for the raw water cooling pump.

- Spark plugs – a complete set.

- Thermostats. Some engines have more than one, so check the manual.

- Belts — at least one spare of each.

- Hoses

- Gasket material and sealant

- PTFE tape

Electrical spares

- Spare crimp of connectors in a variety of sizes.

- Fuses

- De-ionised water for battery top-up (if appropriate)

- Insulating tape

- Petroleum jelly (Vaseline)

Bleeding the fuel system

Much has been said about how forgiving diesels are, but one thing they won't tolerate is air in the fuel system. Air can enter for a number of reasons – running out of fuel or servicing or replacement of components being common causes. Although some engines claim to be self-purging, most need outside intervention.

The exact sequence may vary from engine to engine, but the one described here is typical. It involves filling the system with fuel from tank to injectors, usually by manually operating the lift pump. Simple? Of course!

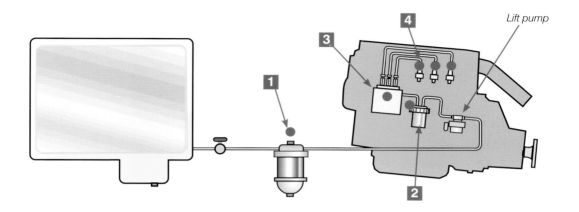

Lift pump

- Ensure the tank has plenty of fuel in it and its shut-off valve is open.

- Try the lift pump's operating handle to see if it works fully. If it doesn't work at all or seems limited, give the engine half a turn (to move the operating cam) and try again.

- If the fuel is drawn from the bottom of the tank and the pre-filter **(1)** is below the level of the fuel, crack open the bleed screw and it will fill by gravity. If not, keep the bleed screw closed – it's time to use the lift pump and turn your attention to the fine filter.

- Open the bleed screw on the fine filter **(2)** and pump away until bubble-free fuel emerges. Don't be astonished if this takes some time. When satisfied, nip up the bleed screw.

This should be enough for most engines, but not for all, including the GM series Yanmars, Perkins, Thorneycrofts and the various Kubota derivatives.

- For them, the next step is the injection pump **(3)**. Loosen its bleed screw (some older rotary injection pumps have two bleed screws and you will have to do both, starting with the lower one) and rejoin your labours on the lift pump. Once the fuel runs clear, close the screw (or screws) and give the lift pump a few more strokes for good measure.

This really should be enough. Try and start the engine in the normal way. If you fail you will have to bleed the injectors. Since these are on the high pressure side of the injection pump, the manual lift pump won't be up to the task, so you will need to use the engine.

- Loosen all the injection pump nuts at the injectors **(4)** a couple of turns.

- Set the throttle to full ahead, out of gear, and turn the engine over with the ignition key. Limit yourself to no more than 15 second bursts to avoid burning out the starter motor.

- First you will see the inevitable bubbles around the nuts, but these will become squirts. At which time, harden down the injector nuts and … start the engine!

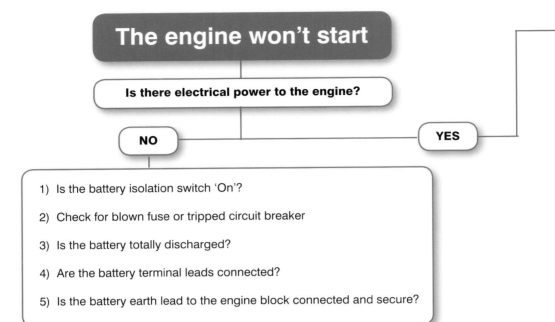

1) Is the battery isolation switch 'On'?

2) Check for blown fuse or tripped circuit breaker

3) Is the battery totally discharged?

4) Are the battery terminal leads connected?

5) Is the battery earth lead to the engine block connected and secure?

1) This is a common but surprisingly easy mistake to make. The usual arrangement is to have a single switch in the positive side of the circuit, but many European boats also isolate the negative side. Both must be switched on for the engine to start.

2) Engine control fuses aren't always easy to find. There may be a small fuse box mounted on the engine block somewhere or – a ridiculous practice on some engines – it could even be wound in beneath the engine wiring loom insulation! You may have to consult the service manual.

3) A battery's voltage doesn't have to be zero for it to be useless. A fully charged 12V battery at rest will show around 12.8V. By the time that reading drops to 10.5V it's effectively 100% flat. If your power management system includes a voltmeter or bar graph type state-of-charge indicator, monitoring the battery condition is very straightforward. If not, you will have to resort to a hydrometer or portable multimeter.

4) Engine starting creates high electrical demands. Any voltage drop due to corroded or loose connections can result in total failure. Check that there's no corrosion and that the terminal clamps are tight on the posts.

5) The same goes for the cable that goes from the battery negative to the engine block. Vibration can easily loosen the connection, so make sure it's clean and nip up the securing bolt.

6) Starter solenoids can draw quite a lot of power. To avoid running heavy cables from the starting switch to the solenoid, a secondary switch known as a 'relay' is often used. Turning the ignition key activates the relay which, in turn, switches on the power to operate the solenoid. Relays are unserviceable items. If defective they should be replaced.

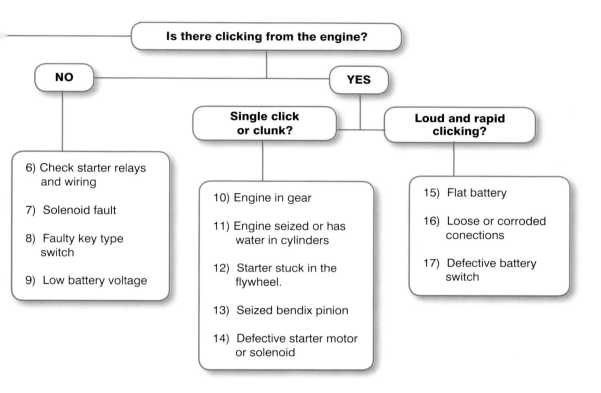

Is there clicking from the engine?

NO

YES

Single click or clunk?

Loud and rapid clicking?

6) Check starter relays and wiring

7) Solenoid fault

8) Faulty key type switch

9) Low battery voltage

10) Engine in gear

11) Engine seized or has water in cylinders

12) Starter stuck in the flywheel.

13) Seized bendix pinion

14) Defective starter motor or solenoid

15) Flat battery

16) Loose or corroded conections

17) Defective battery switch

7) Solenoids sometimes get stuck. They can often be freed by tapping them lightly with the power on. Lightly, mind: DON'T CLOUT IT HARD WITH A HAMMER!

8) Key type switches are notoriously prone to faults. Pushbutton ones are much more reliable. The switch can be bypassed by connecting across the solenoid terminals.

9) If your cabin lights dim when you operate the starting switch, you can be sure that batteries are at a low state of charge. Try switching off all other appliances so the starter motor can have what little power is left.

10) Most engines will start in gear but if the prop is heavily fouled there may be too much resistance.

11) If the water has only been in the engine a short time, you can act to prevent expensive damage. If it has seized, you are almost certainly facing a complete overhaul.

12, 13 & 14) The starter motor should be removed so it can be freed up or sent away for repair.

15) If the engine can't be hand started, there's nothing for it but to find some other means of charging the battery.

16) Clean and tighten as required.

17) Bypass or replace.

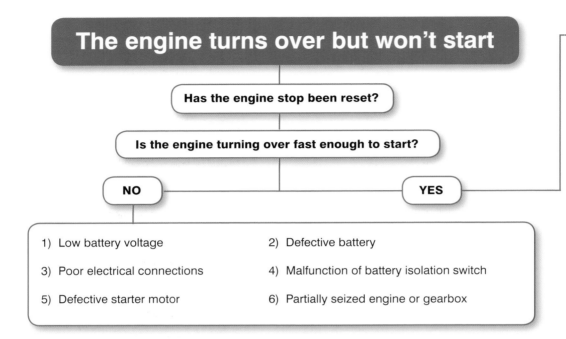

The engine turns over but won't start

Has the engine stop been reset?

Is the engine turning over fast enough to start?

NO | **YES**

1) Low battery voltage	2) Defective battery
3) Poor electrical connections	4) Malfunction of battery isolation switch
5) Defective starter motor	6) Partially seized engine or gearbox

1, 2 & 3) When it comes to engine starting, cranking speed is of the essence. And, since the rotation is usually gained by electrical power, look towards the most obvious causes before suspecting anything more dramatic. If your batteries have deteriorated to the point when they will no longer hold their charge, there's no solution other than replacement. However, there are a couple of tricks that might get you out of trouble. If there are decompression levers on your engine, open them until the speed mounts, then drop them down.

4) Isolating switches are fairly robust by nature, but wear and sparking can damage their internal contacts, thereby increasing resistance. Replacement is the only permanent cure but a temporary fix can be achieved by taking the switch out of the circuit entirely. The easiest way of doing this is to connect both cable terminals to the same connector post on the back of the switch.

5) The field windings could be breaking down or the bearings could be worn or partially seized. If the motor gets very hot to the touch, this is a sure sign that it's drawing lots of current and ailing seriously. It should be reconditioned or replaced.

6) Time for an overhaul.

7) Since tanks usually run dry while the engine is running, it would be very odd indeed if you suddenly found it empty. Check that leak hasn't dumped the fuel into the bilge. And remember: whatever the cause, once everything is shipshape again the system will require bleeding before you can run the engine. See p 96.

8) An easy oversight. You are not alone!

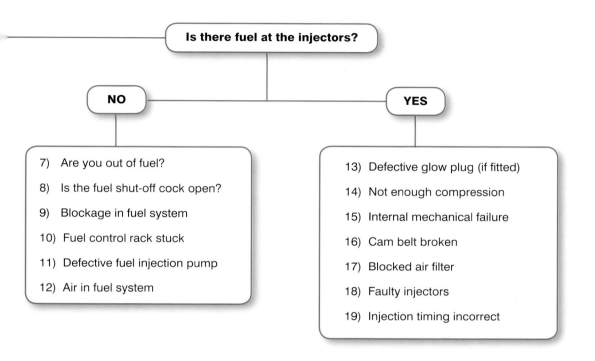

9) The causes of blockage can be many. First check the pre-filter to see if there's anything in the sediment bowl. Then act accordingly.

10 & 11) This is dragon country and none but the most expert should venture inside. Time to get help.

13) The engine is too cold. You may have better luck at a warmer time of day or perhaps you can warm the engine gently by other means – a hot water bottle, for instance.

14) Take off the air filter and aim a couple of squirts of oil as deep into the inlet manifold as possible. The objective is to allow the oil to run down the cylinder walls to help seal the piston rings. Be careful not to overdo it. Oil is incompressible and excessive amounts could damage the engine. As soon as the engine fires, replace the air filter.
This, of course, is only a short term measure. The problem is one of general wear and tear and the need for an overhaul is imminent.

15 & 16) Time to call an engineer.

17) Replace or clean.

18) Replace or send away for servicing.

19) Consult your engine manual. This can be quite a simple job on some engines. If in doubt, call in an engineer.

Chapter 14

OUR OBLIGATIONS TO OTHERS

'MANNERS MAKETH MAN'

These words from William of Wykeham (1324-1404), once bishop of Winchester, summarise an important aspect of seamanship. In the introduction to this book we touched on the bonds that link all mariners, regardless of what sort of vessel they command or crew. When you put to sea you enter a community of fellow seafarers between whom the tradition of 'help thy neighbour' is very strong. Consideration for others is not just simple courtesy, but more a vital ingredient in the code that helps keep all of us as safe as possible.

But courtesy does indeed play its part. Unfortunately there are those who adopt a selfish attitude and, in doing so, spoil it for everyone else.

Sometimes their actions are deliberate and sometimes they arise from ignorance. A considerate skipper will…

- Always match speed to the circumstances. Twenty knots might be fine in clear water but not in narrow channels or anchorages where your wake will rock anchored boats, could swamp or capsize dinghies or send waves crashing onto a nearby beach where children might be playing.

- Be mindful of the manoeuvring limitations of others. Sailing yachts must tack to windward and many can't venture into shallow water. Hopefully they will be just as considerate when they see you have lines in the water which you would prefer not to have snagged.

- Take all rubbish home, and certainly never dump anything that isn't rapidly biodegradable into the sea. Fishing lines can wind around prop shafts and do serious damage to bearings. Nets are even worse.

- Keep a lookout for others who might be in difficulty. An exhausted windsurfer or capsized sailing dinghy probably has no means of signalling distress and could be in very serious danger. Is that man waving from a dory just being friendly or has he run out of fuel? If in doubt, assume the worst and investigate further.

Of course, much of this is just common sense. If we all looked after each other we would need no more than simple rules – the Colregs, for instance – and the rest could be left to human kindness. Well, there's certainly room for that but, just to make sure, many of our responsibilities are spelled out in SOLAS V and have the weight of international law behind them.

In short, consideration for others is more than just being nice – it's a legal obligation that we cannot ignore.

SOLAS V

The letters SOLAS stand for Safety Of Life At Sea and is an international treaty dating back to 1914 in response to the loss of the Titanic. Although primarily intended for merchant ships the regulations apply to all vessels worldwide – and that includes angling boats.

In this summary, the exact wording of the regulations is used with some explanatory notes provided by the RYA.

Radar reflector – Regulation 19.2.1.7.

All ships shall have, if less than 150 gross registered tonnes and if practicable, a radar reflector or other means, to enable detection by ships navigating by radar at both 9 and 3 GHz.

RYA Note: 'When practicable' means that if you can carry a radar reflector, you should. Both passive radar reflectors and active devices are available.

Lifesaving signals – Regulation 29

An illustrated table describing the life-saving signals shall be readily available to the officer of the watch on every ship to which this chapter applies. The signals shall be used by ships or persons in distress when communicating with life-saving stations, maritime rescue units and aircraft engaged in SAR ops.

RYA Note: Keeping this table on board means that you comply with this regulation. The table can be found on pages 105 to 108.

Danger messages – Regulation 31

Masters are to communicate information on navigational dangers. These include, for example, a dangerous derelict or other dangerous obstructions, tropical storms, winds of Force 10 or more for which no warning has been received. The form that information is sent is not obligatory and it can be transmitted in plain language or using the International Code of Signals. Contracting governments must promulgate any danger information received and messages must be free of charge to ships.

RYA Note: This regulation basically means that you, as skipper, have a responsibility to pass on information about navigational dangers to the Coastguard by any means that you can.

Danger messages – Regulation 32

This regulation deals with the kind of information required in danger messages. It also has examples of typical danger messages.

RYA Note: This regulation means that you should pass on sufficient information about navigation dangers you experience or witness (For example: position, nature of danger, time seen/ witnessed, or any other useful information) to enable other shipping in the area to avoid it.

Distress messages – obligations and procedures – Regulation 33

Masters are obliged to respond to distress messages from any source. Ships can be requisitioned by the master of a ship in distress or the Search and Rescue (SAR) authorities.

RYA Note: This regulation reinforces the duty of skippers to respond to any distress messages they hear.

Safe navigation and avoidance of dangerous situations – Regulation 34

Voyage planning is required on all vessels that go to sea. 'Going to sea is defined as proceeding outside of categorized waters'. You can get more information about what constitutes categorized waters from the MCA and the RYA.

MCA guidance notes say for 'small craft and pleasure vessels, the degree of voyage planning will depend on the size of the vessel, its crew and the length of the voyage'. The MCA says that it 'expects all mariners to make a careful assessment of any proposed voyage taking into account all dangers to navigation, weather forecasts, tidal predictions and other relevant factors including the competence of the crew'.

RYA Note: Skippers should note that this regulation changes the status of passage planning on small boats from simply good practice to a requirement under UK law. No formal written plan is required and there is no set format. Anyone who goes on an RYA practical course will be confident of their ability to plan a passage competently. Anyone who is not confident of their passage planning ability should take a suitable RYA practical course.

Misuse of distress signals – Regulation 35

Distress signals should be used for the proper purpose.

RYA Note: This regulation reinforces the fact that distress signals have a life saving role and should not be misused.

LIFE SAVING SIGNALS

These signals are used by ships, aircraft or persons in distress to communicate with rescue service stations, lifeboats, vessels and aircraft engaged in search-and-rescue operations. Use the most suitable signal for the situation and taking into account the prevailing conditions.

Search-and-rescue unit replies

These indicate that you have been seen and assistance will be given as soon as possible.

Orange smoke   **Three white pocket flares**

Surface-to-air signals

These are shown by means of lights or flags or by laying out the symbol on the ground or deck in highly contrasting colours.

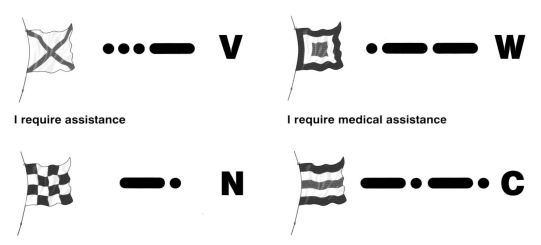

I require assistance   **I require medical assistance**

No or negative   **Yes or affirmative**

Air-to-surface direction signals

Sequence of three manoeuvres meaning **'Go in this direction'**. May be used to show which way to go to assist another vessel or to indicate direction to a safe haven.

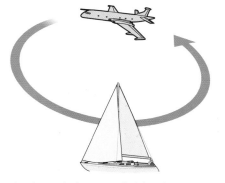

1. plane circles vessel at least once

2. plane crosses low, ahead of boat, rocking wings

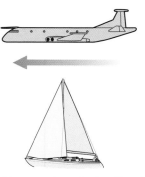

3. plane fl ies over boat in the direction to go

Your assistance is no longer required

Plane crosses low, astern of vessel, rocking wings

Shore-to-ship signals

Safe to land here
Vertical waving of arms, white fl ag, light or fl are.
Morse code letter K – dah dit dah

Landing here is dangerous with additional signals that indicate direction of safer landing place

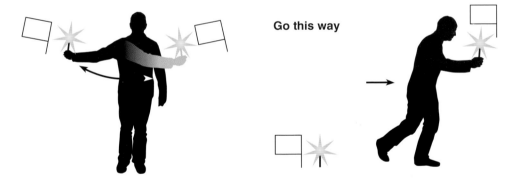

Go this way

Horizontal waving of white fl ag, light or fl are.

Putting one fl ag or fl are on ground and moving in direction of safer landing area with the other indicates direction of safer landing

May also be shown by Morse code light or sound

S – ● ● ●   = landing here is dangerous

R – ● ▬ ●   = land to the right of your current heading

L – ● ▬ ● ●   = land to the left of your current heading

Air-to-surface replies

Message understood

Drop a message

or rocking wings

or flashing landing lights on and off twice

T   **R**

or Morse code by light T = dah   or R = dit dah dit

Message not understood

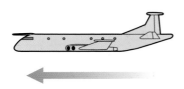

Straight and level flight

or circling

Or morse code by light R P T

R   **P**   **T**

Surface-to-air replies

Message understood – I will comply

Change course to required direction

Or Morse code by light T = ▬▬ or code and answering pendant

I am unable to comply

Morse code by light N = ▬▬● or code flag N

GLOSSARY

ABEAM	Situated to one side of the boat.
AFT	Towards the stern.
AHEAD	In front of the boat.
AMIDSHIPS (MIDSHIPS)	In the middle of the boat. To put the helm amidships is to centre the wheel or tiller so the boat steers straight ahead.
ASTERN	Behind the boat.
BEAM	The maximum width of the boat.
BERTH	A place to moor, or for someone to sleep.
BOLLARD	A strong point to secure a mooring warp, either on the dock or the boat.
BOW	The forward part of the boat. Port and Starboard bows are either side of the stem.
BOW ROLLER	A fairlead for the anchor warp.
BROACH (BROACHING)	An uncontrollable turn into the wind.
CATAMARAN	A boat with two separate hulls.
CATENARY (of warp)	The curve made by the anchor warp between the stem and the anchor.
CLEAT	A 'T' shaped strong point for securing ropes.
COCKPIT	An area open to the weather from where a boat is controlled.
COLREGS.	Colloquial term for the International Regulations for the Prevention of Collision at Sea. IRPCS.
DISPLACEMENT	The weight of water displaced by a vessel afloat.
DISPLACEMENT MODE	When a vessel is operating without benefit of hydrodynamic lift – i.e. not planing.
DOWNTIDE, DOWNSTREAM	To run with the tide or stream.
DSC	Digital Selective Calling. A system whereby a VHF radio transmitter can make an automatic digitized call to a selected station.
FAIRLEAD	A deck fitting used to lead a rope towards a winch or cleat to minimise chafe.
FAIRWAY	The main channel into a harbour. That part of an approach channel lying outside of a harbour entrance.
FENDERS	Soft (often air-filled) pads hung over a boat's sides to protect it from anything alongside.
FREEBOARD	The vertical distance from the waterline to the deck.
HEEL	The amount that a boat leans over.
HELM	The steering position. The tiller or wheel. The person steering (of either gender).

GLOSSARY

HELMSMAN	The person steering a vessel.
IRPCS	See COLREGS.
KNOT	One nautical mile per hour.
LEE SHORE	A shore onto which the wind is blowing.
LEEWARD	The side of the boat facing away from the wind.
MARINA	An sheltered area with berths and other facilities, provided for boaters.
MOB	Man overboard.
PIVOT POINT	The point around which a boat swivels when it is steered.
PLANING	Operating a vessel fast, with the hull skimming over the surface of the water rather than through it.
PONTOON	A floating platform used for mooring boats.
PORT	The left hand side of the boat looking forward.
PORT SIDE TO	Placing the port side of the vessel against a quay or pontoon.
QUARTER	The side of a vessel between amidships and the stern.
RIB	A rigid inflatable boat. Usually a small powerboat.
RODE	Anchor chain or rope or combination of both.
SAR	Search and rescue.
SCREW	Colloquial term for propeller.
SKEG	A fixed fin used to support the leading edge of a rudder.
STARBOARD	The right hand side of a boat looking forward.
STEERAGE WAY	The minimum speed required to maintain control of a boat via the rudder.
STERN	The rear end of a boat.
STREAM	The flow or movement of water, whether caused by current or tide.
TACK	To sail a boat's bow through the wind.
TACKING	The zig-zag course of a boat sailing upwind.
TIDEWAY	Channels where the effects of tidal stream can be felt.
TILLER	A steering bar connected to the rudder.
TOPSIDES	Sides of the boat between the waterline and the deck.
TRANSOM	A flat section of hull across the stern of a boat.
TRIM TABS	Adjustable horizontal plates on the stern of a power boat which help control trim.
UPTIDE	Upstream, running against the flow of water.
WAKE	The trail of disturbed water left behind a moving boat.
WARP	A rope used for mooring or anchoring.
WINDAGE	The amount by which a vessel is affected by wind. Also the areas of hull and superstructure that contribute to this effect.
WINDWARD	The side that the wind is coming from.
WINDWARD BERTH	A berth that a boat is blown away from.

INDEX

INDEX

INDEX

INDEX

RYA *Membership*

Promoting and Protecting Boating
www.rya.org.uk

RYA Membership

The RYA is the national organisation which represents the interests of everyone who goes boating for pleasure.

The greater the membership, the louder our voice when it comes to protecting members' interests.

Apply for membership today, and support the RYA, to help the RYA support you.

BENEFITS OF MEMBERSHIP

- Special members' discounts on a range of products and services including boat insurance, books, charts, DVD's and class certificates
- Access to expert advice on all aspects of boating from legal wrangles to training matters
- Free issue of Certificates of Competence, increasingly asked for by everyone from overseas governments to holiday companies, insurance underwriters to boat hirers
- Access to the wide range of RYA publications,including the quarterly magazine
- Third Party insurance for windsurfing members
- Free Internet access with RYA-Online
- Special discounts on AA membership
- Regular offers in RYA Magazine
- ...and much more

JOIN NOW

Membership form opposite or join online at www.rya.org.uk

Visit our website for information, advice, members' services and web shop.

1 **Important** To help us comply with Data Protection legislation, please tick *either* Box A or Box B (you must tick Box A to ensure you receive the full benefits of RYA membership). The RYA will not pass your data to third parties.

A. I wish to join the RYA and receive future information on member services, benefits and offers by post and email.

B. I wish to join the RYA but do not wish to receive future information on member services, benefits and offers by post and email.

When completed, please send this form to: RYA, RYA House, Ensign Way, Hamble, Southampton, SO31 4YA

2

Title	Forename	Surname	Date of Birth			Male	Female
			D D / M M / Y Y				
1.							
2.							
3.							
4.							

Address

Town   County   Post Code

Evening Telephone   Daytime Telephone

email

3 **Type of membership required:** *(Tick Box)*

☐ **Personal**   *Annual rate £39 or £36 by Direct Debit*

☐ **Under 21**   *Annual rate £13 (no reduction for Direct Debit)*

☐ **Family***   *Annual rate £58 or £55 by Direct Debit*

* Family Membership: 2 adults plus any under 21s all living at the same address

Signature:..................................   Date:..................................

4 Please tick ONE box to show your main boating interest.

☐ Yacht Racing   ☐ Yacht Cruising
☐ Dinghy Racing   ☐ Dinghy Cruising
☐ Personal Watercraft   ☐ Inland Waterways
☐ Powerboat Racing   ☐ Windsurfing
☐ Motor Boating   ☐ Sportsboats and RIBs

Please see Direct Debit form overleaf

Instructions to your Bank or Building Society to pay by Direct Debit

Please complete this form and return it to:
Royal Yachting Association, RYA House, Ensign Way, Hamble, Southampton, Hampshire SO31 4YA

DIRECT Debit

1. To The Manager: _____ Bank/Building Society

   Address: _____

   _____

   Post Code: _____

Originators Identification Number

9	5	5	2	1	3

5. RYA Membership Number (For office use only)

2. Name(s) of account holder(s)

   _____

   _____

3. Branch Sort Code

   | | | — | | | — | | |

4. Bank or Building Society account number

   | | | | | | | | |

6. **Instruction to pay your Bank or Building Society**
   Please pay Royal Yachting Association Direct Debits from the account detailed in this instruction subject to the safeguards assured by The Direct Debit Guarantee.
   I understand that this instruction may remain with the Royal Yachting Association and, if so, details will be passed electronically to my Bank/Building Society.

   Signature(s) _____

   Date _____

Banks and Building Societies may not accept Direct Debit instructions for some types of account

Cash, Cheque, Postal Order enclosed
Made payable to the Royal Yachting Association

£ _____

077   **Office use only:** Membership Number Allocated

Join The Green Blue...

THE GREEN BLUE
MAKING THE ENVIRONMENT SECOND NATURE

...in protecting our coasts and waterways.

Each time we use, clean or maintain our boat we may be harming the beautiful environment we are out to enjoy. The good news is that it there are simple things everyone can do to prevent this. Follow our 'top tips' to ensure that your conscience is as clean as your boat!

EFFECTS ON WILDLIFE
Find out whether the areas you visit are protected and why. There may be vulnerable seabed species, so beware of dragging your anchor.

OIL AND FUEL SPILLS
Good maintenance of fuel lines, connections and seals helps avoid leaks. Check bilge water for contaminants before routine pumping.

ANTIFOULING & MARINE PAINTS
Only scrub off the fouling, not the paint and encourage your marina, club or boatyard to collect & properly dispose of wash down residues.

WASTE MANAGEMENT
Don't throw anything over the side, including food; even orange peel can take up to 2 years to decompose in the water.

RESOURCE EFFICIENCY
The latest generation of wind generators are quiet, efficient and a great way to charge your batteries.

CLEANING AND MAINTENANCE
Replacing acidic teak cleaners with a mild soap and abrasive pad is not only better for the environment but eliminates solvents which may damage seam compounds.

**More tips and advice can be found on our website:
www.thegreenblue.org.uk**

**Read the Environmental Code of Practice to find out how your club can reduce its impact on the environment:
www.ecop.org.uk**

**THE GREEN BLUE
RYA House, Ensign Way,
Hamble, Southampton
SO31 4YA
Tel: 023 8060 4227
www.thegreenblue.org.uk
info@thegreenblue.org.uk**
© Copyright The Green Blue 2007

British Marine Federation

RYA

THE CROWN ESTATE

RYA Training Courses

for all ages, abilities and aspirations

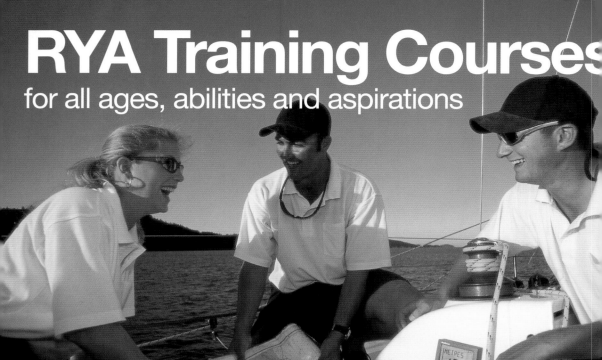

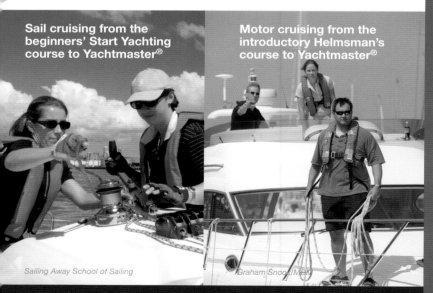

Get the most from your time on the water with our range of practical and shorebased courses.

Sail cruising from the beginners' Start Yachting course to Yachtmaster®

Motor cruising from the introductory Helmsman's course to Yachtmaster®

Sailing Away School of Sailing

Graham Snook/MBM

For further information see www.ryatraining.org, call 00 44 (0)23 8060 4158 for a brochure or email training@rya.org.uk

NOTES